The Strength of Weakness

The Strength of Weakness

Roy Clements

Christian Focus Publications

© 1994 Roy Clements
ISBN 1-85792-073-2

Published by
Christian Focus Publications Ltd
Geanies House, Fearn, Ross-shire,
IV20 1TW, Scotland, Great Britain.

Printed and bound in Great Britain by
The Guernsey Press Co. Ltd, Guernsey, Channel Islands

Cover design by Donna Macleod

Scripture quotations, unless otherwise indicated, are from *The
New International Version*,
published by Hodder and Stoughton

Contents

For the congregation of Eden Baptist Church, Cambridge,
who first heard these chapters as Sunday morning sermons
and to whose patience and encouragement
this preacher owes a very great debt.

Foreword

The Christian world is afflicted with many kinds of bad sermons. Some are racy and interesting, but have only the most marginal connection with the Bible. Others are long on pedantic exegesis and minute detail, but sound rather more like academic lectures than the voice of God addressing lost human beings. Some are more or less orthodox, but are characterised by bombast, not thought. Some are faithful to Scripture and genuinely address human beings, but only the human beings of the 1950s: the preacher has exerted little effort both to understand the times and to address them. But above all, many sermons today, for whatever reason, are ineffably boring: there is no fire, no unction, no grace, no power. Bring on the musicians and the drama groups: at least they enable us to escape boredom.

Mercifully, God never leaves himself without witness. In every generation he raises up particularly gifted teachers and preachers of the Word of God who set a standard of better things and point the way forward.

As much as he will be embarrassed to read these words - the impetus for this Foreword comes from the Publishers, not from him – Roy Clements is one of those people. Of course, there are many unknown preachers who work faithfully at their task. They are unsung heroes, and should not be despised when we offer our thanks to God for the more gifted. But in reality, provided they have escaped the sins of ministerial jealousy, they will be the first to give thanks to God for particularly gifted leaders of the church of God. They not only nourish the people of God, they also set a standard and a model that encourage the rest of us to stretch forward to improve our own service to God.

The sermons in this book are lightly edited versions of the regular ministry at Eden Baptist Church, Cambridge. They will help all who take the Bible seriously not only to understand 2 Corinthians better but also to apply that letter from Paul's hand to us who live at the end of the twentieth century. So Paul, though dead, still speaks; more, God himself speaks – in the words given once for all in a particular time and place and language and culture, and by his Spirit in the renewing application of those words to our own time. Here is instruction, rebuke, correction, call to repentance, edification. Above all, here is powerful exposition of the gospel of God – spiritual nourishment for believers everywhere, and a robust model for preachers who want to improve their own gifts.

D. A. Carson

1

How to View Your Troubles
(2 Corinthians 1:1-11)

Paul, an apostle of Christ Jesus by the will of God, and Timothy our brother,

To the church of God in Corinth, together with all the saints throughout Achaia:

Grace and peace to you from God our Father and the Lord Jesus Christ.

Praise be to the God and Father of our Lord Jesus Christ, the Father of compassion and the God of all comfort, who comforts us in all our troubles, so that we can comfort those in any trouble with the comfort we ourselves have received from God. For just as the sufferings of Christ flow over into our lives, so also through Christ our comfort overflows. If we are distressed, it is for your comfort and salvation; if we are comforted, it is for your comfort, which produces in you patient endurance of the same sufferings we suffer. And our hope for you is firm, because we know that just as you share in our sufferings, so also you share in our comfort.

We do not want you to be uninformed, brothers, about the hardships we suffered in the province of Asia. We were under great pressure, far beyond our ability to endure, so that we despaired even of life. Indeed, in our hearts we felt the sentence of death. But this happened that we might not rely on ourselves but on God, who raises the dead. He has delivered us from such a deadly peril, and he will deliver us. On him we have set our hope that he will continue to deliver us, as you help us by your prayers. Then many will give thanks on our behalf for the gracious favour granted us in answer to the prayers of many (2 Corinthians 1:1-11).

LET ME ASK YOU: WHAT IS YOUR IMAGE OF A GREAT LEADER?

Let me ask you another question: What is your image of a great Christian leader?

Now let me ask you a third question. Did the insertion of the word 'Christian' into the second question materially change your original answer?

For many of us the answer, I suspect, would be 'No'. The qualities we look for in a bishop are much the same as those we look for in a prime minister. We could summarise them in one word: strength. To be a great leader in any context a man or woman must be strong, forceful, tough. The words of great leaders must be trenchant, admitting no contradiction; their actions must be bold, accepting no defeat. They must be people who know how to get their own way; there must be nothing feeble or wimpish about them. There must be no sign of weakness or evidence of failure.

A leader must be somebody whom others can trust without question; so they must project an image as invincible as the *Bismarck* and as infallible as the Pope. That was, for example, the image of Margaret Thatcher when Prime Minister of Britain: she exuded self-assurance and strength. But somebody like George Bush who in many aspects of his presidency possessed a much less assertive and pontifical manner, received public criticism, disillusion and finally rejection precisely because he seemed vulnerable to the charge of weakness.

If that is the way political leaders are perceived, it is even more true of leaders of churches. They too are expected to be strong. Pastors are not allowed to be nervous. They are not allowed to be tired. Others may be overwhelmed by personal problems, but a minister always copes–and he has ample resources left over to help others to cope as well. After all, a Christian leader, like Hercules, is on the side of the gods; so even the queen of the Amazons should be unable to resist his supernaturally-assisted heroics.

That, at any rate, is the myth. But of course, it is only a myth.

I believe that Paul's central purpose in his second letter to the Corinthians is to expose to us the fallacy of that myth: that he is saying to us, 'You are wrong to base your ideas of Christian leadership on the models you derive from your secular culture. Christian leadership is altogether different. Great Christian leaders are not necessarily strong at all, at least not in the way we usually mean that word. On the contrary, it is the primary qualification of any man or woman who is going to be mightily used by God that they should be painfully aware of their inadequacies, and their incompetence.'

That is why I have given this series of studies a title which is a paradox: *The Strength of Weakness*. It is a paradox we are going to encounter again and ag.' n as we make our way through the chapters of this book. It will find its climax when we come to Chapter 12, where Paul states baldly: 'When I am weak, then I am strong.'

1. The Background to Paul's Letter

What were the circumstances that lie behind this letter and determine its central theme?

You can read in the book of Acts how Paul founded the church in Corinth during his missionary travels. From the very beginning of his ministry there he suffered a great deal of opposition, particularly from the influential Jewish community that lived in that commercial metropolis. After a period of some eighteen months he moved on into Asia, eventually settling in Ephesus for a number of years. But the troubles in Corinth did not cease when he left. There was false teaching. There was sexual immorality. There was a very unpleasant divisiveness in the fellowship.

As a result, Paul wrote two letters to the church in Corinth. The first has not come down to us. Paul refers to it in the second letter he wrote (which, confusingly, we know as 1 Corinthians).

Unfortunately the correspondence does not seem to have resolved the problems in Corinth; or, if it did, new problems just as serious arose later. For Paul followed up the two letters with a personal visit, and found the situation in the church as unsatisfactory as ever. A group of outsiders seemed to have risen to dominance. The question of who exactly these outsiders were has generated a good deal of study and even more ingenuity among New Testament commentators; but the truth is that we do not know. It is very difficult to identify them with any known heresy or movement in the early church. All we can say with reasonable confidence is that they were Jews; that they dignified themselves with the title 'apostle'; and – most important of all – that their ideas of Christian leadership were very different from those of Paul.

They believed, just as we today are inclined to believe, that great Christian leaders should be impressive, forceful, strong personalities. And I suspect they believed it for the same reason that we tend to believe it: because it was the prevailing leadership model in the secular Hellenistic world from which they came.

The ancient Greeks were characterised by huge admiration for success. In their culture, whether you were an orator or an athlete, an actor or a soldier, the important thing was that you should succeed. At the centre of all their philosophy and religion was the cult of the hero. If one wished to advance in Hellenistic society, that was the kind of high-powered image that one had to project: eloquent, confident, achieving, virile – in a word, strong. In Paul's time there were even itinerant teachers called Sophists who made their living by giving ambitious youths tuition in the necessary skills and virtues by which they could nurture that kind of impressive persona; rather like the advertisements you can read in newspapers today offering courses by which the shy and ineffectual can improve their self-confidence and succeed in their careers. And there seems to be something more than a little sophistical about this group of outsiders who had invaded the church in Corinth, not least their interest in professional fees for their services.

These self-styled 'apostles' offered to the Christians at Corinth the kind of strong leadership which the secular world of that day admired. But in so doing, they clashed with Paul. We shall see in our next study that Paul described his visit to Corinth as an immensely painful one; so much so that he could not bring himself to visit them again as he had planned to do. Instead, he wrote at least one other letter, probably more than one; and it is from this additional correspondence that the letter that we know as 2 Corinthians is derived.

Unlike 1 Corinthians, this letter has little to say on moral or theological issues. If the members of the opposition party in Corinth were sexually permissive, or were teaching heresy of some kind, Paul says very little about it. It is neither his doctrine nor his ethics that he perceives to be the principal object of their attack. It is his understanding of Christian leadership that they were contradicting. They aspired to project an image of strength; Paul was content to project an image of weakness. The result was they despised Paul. They ridiculed him, they derogated him as a charlatan. 'Call him an apostle?' they said. 'He is no apostle, he is a clown.'

Yet Paul knew in his heart of hearts that it was he, not they, who represented real apostleship. They took their inspiration for leadership from the spirit of the age; he took his inspiration from the Spirit of God. They drew their examples for leadership from the secular messiahs of their day; he took his from the Lord Jesus Christ himself. And as we study this letter we shall learn a lot about Christian leadership as a result of this controversy between Paul and his rivals. We shall learn it as we hear Paul, uncharacteristically and not without a good deal of personal embarrassment at times, defending his leadership style and leadership credentials against these rivals who wanted to impugn them.

I believe that they are vitally important lessons for all of us, even if we do not exercise formal leadership in the church. For we all, in informal ways, function as leaders. After all, leadership reduced to its simplest element simply means the power to influence other people. And we all do that, even if it is only our children, or our younger brother or sister, or our marriage partner, or our friends; we all have people who look to us for direction, we all have the power to influence. And the question that Paul is anxious for us to ask ourselves in this second letter to the Corinthians is this: What kind of leadership image do you want to project as a Christian? How important to you is it that people should perceive you as strong?

2. Paul's Troubles

We begin with a lesson about troubles. We all have troubles, of course, but how do we view them? How honest are we prepared to be about them? Paul was willing to be extremely honest about his:

> **We do not want you to be uninformed, brothers, about the hardships we suffered in the province of Asia. We were under great pressure, far beyond our ability to endure, so that we despaired even of life. Indeed, in our hearts we felt the sentence of death** (1:8-9).

Clearly Paul's experiences since leaving Corinth for Asia had been deeply disturbing, though it is impossible to know for certain what kind of trouble he had encountered. The book of Acts indicates that there was a good deal of anti-Christian hostility in Ephesus, even extending to an organised public demonstration by Trade Unionists against Paul in the city square. He spoke in his first letter to Corinth of 'fighting with wild beasts at Ephesus' and said that many there opposed him. So it is not unlikely that the 'great pressure' of which he speaks in verse 8 was the result of an intensification of this atmosphere of persecution. Indeed, the phrase 'sentence of death' (verse 9) could be understood quite literally, as a judicial decree of capital punishment which Paul was expecting any day to receive.

But it is equally possible that Paul is referring to some kind of serious physical sickness. In Chapter 12 he speaks of a 'thorn in the flesh' that would not go away. That is not the usual way of speaking about persecution. His choice of the perfect tense in 1:9 suggests that the sentence of death was not a momentary peril, that had passed as persecution might pass, but a continuing threat to his welfare such as a chronic illness represents. Indeed, you might even argue that when he says 'in our hearts' Paul is literally referring to an internal rather than an external threat to his well-being.

Commentators disagree over exactly what the danger was that Paul faced. But whatever it was, in these verses he goes out of his way to emphasise the gravity of the problem and the depth of private despair to which it had reduced him. 'We were weighed down,' he says (that is the literal translation), 'far beyond our ability to endure', a phrase that implies quite extraordinary and extreme trial. 'We despaired even of life', again, a very vivid word, implying that he could see absolutely no way out. He was at his wits end, at the end of his tether. The very jaws of death seemed to be closing in on him, and, Paul candidly admits, as a result he was at the very point of giving up all hope of survival: 'In our hearts we felt the sentence of death'. Or, as J. B. Phillips bluntly translates it, 'We told ourselves, This is the end.'

I find myself asking this question. Given the background that we have just considered and the fact that Paul is anxious to address his main theme of leadership credibility, why should he, as soon as he puts pen to paper, plunge into an account of these recent troubles? What relevance do they have? Why does he stress so outspokenly the extremes of depression and helplessness to which these troubles have brought him?

It has been suggested that it is a calculated ploy to win the sympathy of the Corinthians; after all, it is hard to criticise a man who has just stood on the brink of martyrdom. So, it is argued, Paul is somewhat magnifying his recent trials in order to regain the respect of the Corinthians and perhaps score a point against his unpersecuted and no doubt well-heeled rivals.

It is a possible explanation, but I want to suggest an alternative one that I find more likely.

It would not be at all surprising if rumours of Paul's hardships had already filtered back to Corinth. That would explain why he did not feel the need to spell out in detail precisely what had happened: they already knew. And so when he says, 'We don't want you to be uninformed,' he is saying: 'Look, I want to be quite open and frank with you about this; I want you to have the whole story.' For it is quite possible too that knowledge of the trouble that Paul was in was being used by his opponents to discredit him. It is not difficult to imagine how those unscrupulous critics could misrepresent the suffering of Paul for their own purposes. 'Look at him, he's given up; we've heard he is sitting in prison morbidly telling everybody he's finished!'

'What kind of a leader is this?', they demand: real leaders never despair; real leaders never get depressed. They triumph over their persecutors, they do not surrender to them in this cowardly fashion.

What is more, if the trial that Paul speaks of was a physical illness rather than persecution, it would have been even easier to pursue this rich line of defamatory gossip. For the Greeks despised physical weakness of any sort. Greek heroes were never ill. They were always portrayed as specimens of bodily perfection. As for the Jews, many of them believed that illness was a sign of divine disfavour. Men who had real spiritual power healed sickness, they never suffered from it. How plausible then, to portray Paul as a pathetic invalid, deserving at best the pity of the Corinthians, and at worst, their contempt!

Of course some people would become defensive under that kind of attack. They would attempt to minimise the seriousness of the trouble they had experienced. 'Oh, you probably heard about that little problem I had in Ephesus. It was nothing really, a mere flea-bite much exaggerated in the Christian press. I was never really upset by it, you know!' But Paul does not play it down like that. He *could not* do so, because it would not have been honest; he had been in a bad spot and he had felt utterly desperate about it. That was the truth. But even more to the point, Paul *would not* play down his troubles in that way and thereby evade his critics, because his understanding of Christian leadership did not require him to. His rivals may have felt it necessary to project an image of personal invincibility in order to support their claims to apostleship, but Paul did not. Unlike them, he was not ashamed of his weakness. He understood the paradox, 'When I am weak, I am strong.'

And so, it seems to me, in this very first chapter of his letter Paul puts that paradox on the agenda for discussion by means of his personal testimony. 'Yes, I was in trouble, bad trouble. Yes, I was in despair; deep despair. But what you Corinthians must realise is that that kind of experience, far from being inconsistent with Christian leadership, is the very stuff from which real Christianity is made.' And to prove his point he gives in these opening verses some positive features of his troubles; insights, if you like, which explain why he viewed his troubles not as tokens of Christian defeat, but as badges of Christian honour.

(a) Christian troubles create a community feeling (1:3-4)

It is not unusual for a New Testament letter to open on a note of doxology with the words 'Praise be to God'. But wherever it occurs it strikes a very Jewish note, because that is how a synagogue liturgy usually began. It may be that Paul is thus subtly establishing his Jewish credentials in the face of his Jewish rivals who probably questioned his Hebrew pedigree as well as everything else about him. There is no doubt that the Jewish flavour is deliberately introduced, for Paul goes on to develop it with several more phrases in these early verses. For example, the phrase 'the Father of compassion' (literally: Father of mercies) preserves the plural of the Hebrew expression rather than using the far more natural singular. Again, the frequently-repeated word 'comfort', used in the sense Paul is using it – 'consolation', 'deliverance from trouble' – has many reverberations from its Old Testament usage, particularly the book of Isaiah where the prophet constantly speaks of how God comforts Zion in her destitution and misery.

Perhaps Paul is very gently reminding his readers, by beginning in this way, that the Old Testament writers were not strangers to the kind of trouble that he had experienced, nor were they shy about publicly admitting how deeply disheartened they had been by it. Think of those psalms where David complains to God about his hopeless situation. Or think of all those desperate appeals from exiles in Babylon to the mercy of God. But think too of all those glorious testimonies to deliverance that they composed in the wake of such trials: 'He lifted me out of the slimy pit ... this poor man called and the LORD heard him and saved him out of all his troubles ... Burst into songs of joy together, you ruins of Jerusalem, the LORD has comforted his people.' That vocabulary, Paul reminds the Corinthians, is familiar to you: and that is how I feel about things.

And I am no more ashamed to say so than those Old Testament saints were. 'Yes, I was in trouble, deep trouble; but the Lord has comforted me, just as he did David, and just as he did the exiles. Like them, I am in a position now to assist others when they go through dark days, by my psalm of testimony. He comforts us in our troubles, so we can comfort those in any trouble with the comfort we ourselves have received from him.'

It is always so. It is a general truth. Trouble has a way of binding human beings together in a way that prosperity never does. Even when the trouble is no more severe than bad weather or a cancelled train at the railway station, people suddenly talk to one another to share their mutual frustration. It is much more so when we are bereaved or seriously ill. We want visitors, we want company. We feel the need for others to support us, to console us. And what a relief it is to hear someone say in that situation, 'You know, I have experienced the very same thing! I know exactly how you feel; it has happened to me too.'

'Well,' says Paul, 'I realise that God put me through this dreadful time of peril precisely so that I might have just such a ministry of encouragement. God's comfort has not been given to me in a bucket for my selfish enjoyment; it has been given to me in a pipe so that I can pass it on to other people. Indeed that is what the words "sympathy" and "compassion" literally mean: "suffering with". But no such shared feeling is really possible except on the basis of shared experience. Those Christian leaders you have got in Corinth, who never admit to having troubles - they may be superficially very impressive, but I tell you that they make very bad pastors. For only those who can testify to the way God has helped them in deep distress can have any real ministry to the distressed in their congregation.'

It may be that this is something we all need to think about. Perhaps you are inclined to think that your Christian life has been a mess, and to brood on all your problems. Perhaps you compare yourself unfavourably with church leaders for whom nothing seems ever to go wrong. You are so aware of your inadequacies that you are sure you could never be like them; you could never be a counsellor.

But have you ever considered that perhaps those same inadequacies and problems of which you are so painfully aware are the very qualifications that God is looking for? There is a leadership strength that can only be acquired through weakness. When we realise that, we will be able to see our troubles in a very different light.

(b) Christian troubles link us with the experience of Jesus himself (1:5)

Read verse 5 very carefully: 'For just as the sufferings of Christ flow over into our lives, so also through Christ our comfort overflows.' It is a very bold expression. What could Paul mean by it? He may have been persecuted or sick - but he had not been crucified; and if he had been, he could hardly have claimed that any cross he could bear would have the same saving significance as the one Jesus died on. Yet this thought of participation in the suffering of Christ is one we encounter regularly in Paul's letters; he even says in Philippians that it is part of his greatest ambition to know 'the fellowship of Christ's sufferings.' What can he mean by it?

I would suggest two facets of Paul's meaning, and neither excludes the other. One is that *Paul sees any suffering that a Christian endures* (especially if endured voluntarily and as a consequence of Christian discipleship) *as a kind of mystical extension of the sufferings of Christ.* After all, Paul speaks of the church as the body of Christ, so any injury inflicted on the church is inflicted on Jesus too. Jesus virtually said as much to Paul when he spoke to him that very first time on the Damascus road: 'Why do you persecute –not the Christians, but –me?' I believe that Paul's understanding of that close union between the church and Jesus in suffering probably originates right there.

But there is a second facet which I think is often overlooked. It may be that *Paul is speaking here not simply of the sufferings of Jesus as an individual, but* (if translated a little more precisely) *the sufferings of 'the Christ', the Messiah.* In Jewish thought tribulation was anticipated as an inescapable component in the experience of God's people, as they lived through the transition between this age and the Messianic age to come. There was a great tribulation in between. So it is not impossible that the phrase 'sufferings of the Christ' could almost be a technical term for that Messianic tribulation of which both the Old Testament prophets and the New Testament apostles spoke, a tribulation which they often said was like the pain of a woman in labour. It would be intense while it lasted, but it would give way to the comfort of the new Messianic age, the comfort that the prophets had spoken of, the comfort of the Christ.

When we take both facets together we see that Paul is attributing enormous dignity to Christian suffering. For Paul the sufferings of Jesus on the cross were a sign of the birth of the new age, a beacon announcing the arrival of the kingdom of God. Therefore the sufferings of Christians, the people of Jesus, can in some circumstances at least share in that same significance. As the people of God living through the last days, we have the privilege of experiencing in our lives, the fulfilment of Messianic prophecy, the tribulation of which it speaks, and the consolation of which it speaks. It is all coming true in us! And so, Paul argues, a link is established between our experience and that of Jesus himself, because our sufferings are a kind of 'referred pain', issuing out of his cross to all who are joined to him in his body. And our comfort? That is a kind of 'referred joy', flowing out of his resurrection through the same channels of spiritual union.

Paul is really saying that he sees his suffering and subsequent deliverance in Asia as an echo – even a recapitulation – in his own experience, of what Good Friday and Easter meant for Jesus and for the world.

That is an astonishing thing to say. No wonder he was not embarrassed to admit the intensity of his trials, or the depth of his anguish. Were not Jesus' sufferings intense? Was not his anguish profound? 'Those so-called apostles may boast that they cope with all their problems, that their difficulties could never bring them to the pitch of despair that I reached,' says Paul. 'Well – if that is so, then all they are really telling us is that they know very little about the Christ.'

This too is something that we would do well to ponder very deeply today. There is a spirit of what some call 'triumphalism' sweeping through certain sections of the church today. Its message is one of health and wealth for all. If you are sick you should claim healing: we should expect such miracles as a regular feature of Christian living. If you are poor you should pray for more money, for it is God's will that every Christian should be materially prosperous. So we read in the Christian press of a woman in Scotland driven to a nervous breakdown because her local fellowship claimed that the miscarriage she had suffered was the result of her lack of faith; and a man in London, rebuked by his church and told that his failure to find employment was the result of hidden sin in his life.

I am quite prepared to accept that some of us expect too little from God. I am quite prepared to admit that perhaps I am not as open as I should be to miraculous answers to my prayers. But I have to say that this kind of prosperity teaching labours under a tragic theological shortcoming. It leaves no place for the cross in a believer's life. According to Paul in these verses, the comfort of Christ in Christian experience is inescapably coupled to the sufferings of Christ, and you cannot expect to enjoy the former without being willing to endure the latter. It is all part of that paradox that Paul will not cease to drum into our minds: strength for the Christian is the corollary, not the opposite, of weakness. We can be raised only when we have first been willing to die.

(c) Christian troubles have a purpose

Now Paul turns to the third fact that enables him to accept his troubles without being ashamed of them.

(1) Suffering helps others (1:6)

The question people almost always ask when trouble comes is: 'Why? Why has this happened to me?' Even atheists ask it, which is in fact remarkable because it means they are much closer to faith in God than they think. If atheists really believed the world was ruled by chance collisions of atoms, the question 'Why?' would never occur to any of them. Yet there is a profound intuition in all human beings that suffering demands an explanation. But what that explanation might be eludes the vast majority of us. Indeed, it eluded the people of God for hundreds of years; all through the Old Testament period, suffering remained a great enigma. Why did God allow innocent people to suffer? Job wrestled with that dilemma but found no answer, except perhaps a slap on the wrist for impertinence! The problem of suffering is posed in the Old Testament but never solved. And yet the interesting thing is that when we come to the New Testament the apostles seem to talk as if all theological difficulties associated with suffering have disappeared. Suffering has ceased to be a problem, and has become instead a vocation. 'To this you were called,' says Peter. 'Christ suffered for you, leaving you an example that you should follow in his steps.'

So what was so special about the sufferings of Jesus that would enable Christians to see their sufferings in a positive rather than a negative light? Surely the key is this: The sufferings of Jesus were sufferings with a purpose. Jesus' death on the cross achieved something. That is the burden of the New Testament message. It was not a pointless gesture; something wonderful was accomplished on that cross, it achieved salvation for men and women. Consequently, Christians living in the light of that cross have the enormous advantage of being able to interpret their own sufferings within that framework of divine purpose. 'God works all things for good,' they could now say without any reservations - because of the cross. And that is how Paul had learned to interpret his own recent trials; he saw God achieving something through them. He has already referred to part of that achievement in verse 4, but in verse 6 he spells it out again: 'Some participation in the tribulation of Christ is the common lot of all God's people: you Corinthians as well as me. And the example of my sufferings and my subsequent deliverance, will therefore be used by God to encourage you to hold fast when the time comes for you to have your share of troubles.'

That is the first thing Paul's suffering achieved. It strengthened the people of God.

And it is true, few things inspire Christian hearts more than stories of those who have passed through trial; often immensely moving stories like Richard Wurmbrand's *Tortured for Christ*, or the story of Joni Eareckson's battle against physical handicap. We can never underestimate the power of a single such testimony to strengthen the church, when it comes from a man or a woman who has endured suffering. I hate that cliché, that is sometimes used — 'He's laid aside on his bed of sickness' — as if the fact that a servant of Christ is ill means that he is temporarily useless to the Master. What nonsense! Those who understand what Paul is saying here may dare to believe that it is precisely when they feel at their weakest that their usefulness as God's servants may be at its strongest.

(2) Suffering helps the one who suffers (1:8-9)

But Paul's suffering achieved more, for he tells us that he himself was benefited by it too. 'This happened,' he explains, 'that we might not rely on ourselves, but on God who raises the dead.' The collapse of his hope and the exposure of his human weakness which the terrible threat against his life produced was, while it may have implied humiliating failure on his part, a singular blessing nevertheless. Paul is convinced that his descent into abject despair was deliberately engineered by God's providence. 'God wanted to teach me to trust in him, rather than in myself.'

What an important lesson that is. Many people think that the opposite of faith is doubt, but they could not be more mistaken. As often as not, doubt is a staging-post on the way to faith. Doubt, uncertainty and intellectual insecurity are experiences we have to pass through to discover faith. The opposite of faith, according to Paul, is not doubt at all, but confidence 'in the flesh'. Confidence that one can cope on one's own; confidence that one does not need the grace of God, thank you very much. Confidence that even under those cruel bludgeonings of chance and the fell clutch of circumstance, still declares:

> My head is bloody but unbow'd ...
> I am the master of my fate;
> I am the captain of my soul.[1]

The people who are farthest from faith are not those who doubt, but those who are all too sure of themselves. Paul could easily have been like that, because by nature he was a self-assured, self-sufficient individual; and human nature being what it is, even after his conversion those personality traits were not totally erased. God had to teach even him, the great apostle, not to rely on himself, but 'on God who raises the dead'.

Put yourself in Paul's shoes for a moment. You are quite convinced you are going to die within the next few days. You are a man in a condemned cell on Death Row. You can almost see the noose hanging from the ceiling over your head. Certainly, before that experience Paul believed in a God who raised the dead — but do you not think he believed in such a God in an altogether more real and existential way after it? You bet your life he did! Indeed, betting his life was what the experience was all about.

I suspect that the vital living faith that God wants to form in us always remains untried and virtually hypothetical in our lives until we are similarly brought to a sense of helplessness. Real faith can only be constructed on the ruins of our own self-despair. That is why people do not like the gospel. It is all too easy to put your hand up at an evangelistic meeting, or to give your testimony at the youth club, or even to be baptised. But the challenge of the New Testament is this: 'Be a believer unto death, and I will give you a crown of life.'

Of course troubles have a purpose. If it were not for troubles, dreadful troubles that bring people down to the very bottom, I wonder if there would be any faith worth the name in this world at all. But even that does not exhaust the purposes achieved by Paul's suffering.

---

1. W E Henley, 'Invictus'.

(3) Christian troubles teach Christians to pray (1:10-11)

Paul did not believe that the danger was past. He felt he needed a continuing deliverance, if he was going to avoid the chasm of death that had opened at his feet. And he is convinced, in verses 10-11, that the corporate prayer life of the church had a vital role in sustaining that divine mercy, or, as he calls it, 'that gracious favour' that had been granted to him.

The phrase 'you will help us by your prayers' is a rather dull translation of a very rich word. If you separate the word into its component elements it means that prayer is a labour in which we all collaborate together to support somebody else. And that is precisely how Paul saw it. Nothing motivates the prayer life of the church like the knowledge of a fellow Christian in trouble. Think of how the early church prayed when they heard that Peter had been arrested; and in very recent times, the news of an accident to a child within my own church family brought new urgency to the prayer-meeting. It has always been so. And what is the effect of this corporate intercession? It not only increases the praying, eventually it increases the thanksgiving. 'Then many will give thanks on our behalf for the gracious favour granted in answer to the prayers of many.'

The expression Paul uses is a rather interesting one. Literally, it means that the thanksgiving will ascend to God from 'many faces'. He could simply mean 'many persons', which is a common use of the word, or he might be visualising many faces upturned towards God in prayer. But I rather like the suggestion that he may have at the back of his mind the Greek use of the word 'face' to mean an actor in a play. It is as if he is saying, 'Through this corporate prayer, you are getting actively involved in the drama of my suffering. So when the final curtain falls and the cast take their bow, instead of there being just one person on the stage – me, Paul – you are all going to be there too, adding your voices to the thanksgiving and the glory which flow to God because of my deliverance. It is all going to be multiplied because you played such an intercessory role.'

And perhaps from God's point of view that is the most satisfying achievement of all.

3. How to view your troubles

How then should we view our troubles?

Most definitely, we should not view them with resentment, as if they ought not to happen to us; still less with embarrassment, as if they cast some slur on our Christian spirituality. Trouble, Paul explains, is part of our normal Christian experience, binding God's people together in mutual dependence and concern, generating ministries of encouragement and consolation among us. It is how God links us with the very experience of Jesus himself. We have the huge privilege as the people of the Messiah to participate in his tribulations, the tribulations that bring in his kingdom. And (perhaps most encouraging of all) troubles in a Christian's life have a purpose for the life of the people of God generally, a purpose in our own lives individually, and a purpose that will even enrich the life of heaven through multiplying the prayer and the gratitude which surround the throne of God. That is why Browning is right when he says, 'Welcome each rebuff that turns earth's smoothness rough'; that is why James is right when he says, 'Count it all joy when you fall into various trials' (James 1:2).

Do not misunderstand me. Paul is not giving support here to the kind of stiff upper lip stoic who pretends that pain does not hurt. He does not welcome suffering; he is not a masochist. Nor does he condone the kind of indulgent self-pity that Charles Dickens' Mrs Gummidge wallows in. He is utterly frank about the trauma that suffering brings. He did not enjoy his spell on death row. And nothing in his Christianity required him to pretend that he did.

And yet there is a sense in which he was glad it had happened. For God had done things in his life and in other people's lives as a result of it, and he wanted the Corinthians to understand that. Great leader though he was, he wanted them to realise that leadership did not elevate him into some kind of elite, where weakness and failure are unknown. On the contrary, being an apostle had led Paul into greater depths of self-doubt, greater and more humiliating awareness of his own inadequacy than he would ever have believed possible. If being a leader means projecting the image of a strong man who never gets depressed, never finds circumstances too much for him, is never afraid to die, then Paul was no leader. But he had learned enough from his Master to realise that Christian leadership has nothing to do with that kind of so-called strength.

As for those so-called apostles, who reckoned that weakness was a disqualification, I suspect that he had nothing but pity for them. In their super-spiritual triumphalism, they really did not know what they were missing.

2

Love Hurts
(2 Corinthians 1:12-2:11)

Now this our boast: Our conscience testifies that we have conducted ourselves in the world, and especially in our relations with you, in the holiness and sincerity that are from God. We have done so not according to worldly wisdom but according to God's grace. For we do not write you anything you cannot read or understand. And I hope that, as you have understood us in part, you will come to understand fully that you can boast of us just as we will boast of you in the day of the Lord Jesus.

Because I was confident of this, I planned to visit you first so that you might benefit twice. I planned to visit you on my way to Macedonia and to come back to you from Macedonia, and then to have you send me on my way to Judea. When I planned this, did I do it lightly? Or do I make my plans in a worldly manner so that in the same breath I say, "Yes, yes" and "No, no"?

But as surely as God is faithful, our message to you is not "Yes" and "No". For the Son of God, Jesus Christ, who was preached among you by me and Silas and Timothy, was not "Yes" and "No," but in him it has always been "Yes". For no matter how many promises God has made, they are "Yes" in Christ. And so through him the "Amen" is spoken by us to the glory of God. Now it is God who makes both us and you stand firm in Christ. He anointed us, set his seal of ownership on us, and put his Spirit in our hearts as a deposit, guaranteeing what is to come.

I call God as my witness that it was in order to spare you that I did not return to Corinth. Not that we lord it over your faith, but we work with you for your joy, because it is by faith you stand firm. So I made up my mind that I would not make another painful visit to you. For if I grieve you, who is left to make me glad but you whom I have grieved? I wrote as I did so that when I came I should not be distressed by those who ought to make me rejoice. I had confidence in all of you, that you would all share my joy. For I wrote you out of great distress and anguish of heart and with many tears, not to grieve you but to let you know the depth of my love for you.

If anyone has caused grief, he has not so much grieved me as he has grieved all of you, to some extent—not to put it too severely. The punishment inflicted on him by the majority is sufficient for him. Now instead, you ought to forgive and comfort him, so that he will not be overwhelmed by excessive sorrow. I urge you, therefore, to reaffirm your love for him. The reason I wrote you was to see if you would stand the test and be obedient in everything. If you forgive anyone, I also forgive him. And what I have forgiven—if there was anything to forgive—I have forgiven in the sight of Christ for your sake, in order that Satan might not outwit us. For we are not unaware of his schemes (2 Corinthians 1:12-2:11).

'THIS IS GOING TO HURT ME MORE THAN IT HURTS YOU!', SAYS THE FATHER, REACHING FOR HIS SLIPPER.

If some people had their way, those words would constitute evidence for the prosecution in a trial at the European Court of Justice. They argue that sane, caring and responsible parents would never wish to inflict pain on their children. Yet I suspect that most people who have received the occasional caning in their youth would regard the issues as not so clear-cut. Without doubt, sadistic parents exist who victimise the children in their care and thoroughly deserve to be punished in the court for their cruelty. But for the vast majority of fathers who ever raised a hand against their children, that old cliché is true: it did hurt them more than it hurt their offspring. If it were not so (though the child might be excused a certain scepticism on the point), then the chastisement would have had little effect except to provoke resentment and hostility in the child.

It is vital, if children are going to develop into responsible and well-adjusted adults, that they perceive any punishment they receive – corporal or otherwise – as an act of love rather than of arbitrary vengeance. That is why the home is so much more important to the moral welfare of our society than the classroom or the civil courts could ever be, no matter how enlightened their jurisprudence or their educational methods might be. Remedial training is only possible in the context of a circle of caring relations such as the family provides. The state may be able to avenge crime, it may be able to some extent to deter crime; but (unless it is prepared to use the most vicious forms of psychological manipulation) there is very little it can do to change criminals. For no matter how paternalistic our schools or prisons may try to be, they simply lack that interpersonal love which alone can turn retributive punishment into corrective discipline.

That is why I have to confess that I am somewhat saddened by the campaign for the abolition of corporal punishment. It is not, I hasten to say, because I want to beat my children. But such a move represents an erosion of parental authority which were better left undisturbed. He who spares the rod, hates his son, said wise Solomon (Proverbs 13:24) – a philosophy undoubtedly open to abuse, but not surely so morally repugnant that it has to be proscribed by statutory ban.

I want to suggest to you that there are times when love must inflict pain on the loved one, for love's sake. The acid test as to whether it is love, rather than some less noble motive that is at work, is as simple as that old adage with which we began: This is going to hurt me more than it hurts you. Whenever love causes pain, it always does so like a boomerang: reciprocally. That is why I have called this chapter 'Love Hurts'. There is an ambiguity in those two words. Love hurts –yes, there are occasions when love must be a little cruel to be kind; the failure to administer such benevolent pain is not love at all but mere sentimentality. But whenever love feels it necessary to hurt in that way, it feels the pain even more intensively than the loved one upon whom the hurt was directly inflicted. 'This is going to hurt me more than it hurts you.' That is the truth, I suggest, of all loving discipline.

Nobody understood it better than the apostle Paul. He loved the church at Corinth. For eighteen months he had worked among them as their pastor, and an intense bond of affection had grown up between him and the congregation. He was as proud of that Corinthian church as a father is proud of his children. Yet fond though he was of them, he had had to rebuke them. Things were going on in the congregation which could not be tolerated in a Christian church, and Paul felt it necessary to write a very stiff letter to them on the subject. Of course the Corinthians felt hurt in consequence, and Paul felt hurt that he had had to hurt them.

Even so, had the close relationship between the Corinthians and Paul been allowed to re-establish itself, had the situation been allowed to calm down, I have no doubt that the crisis would have quickly blown over. The warm family feeling that united the church with their founding father would have blossomed afresh very quickly. Unfortunately, the healing process that should have followed Paul's rebuke was not allowed to proceed. It was interrupted by the invasion of the Corinthian church by the group of outsiders we have already described – strong, persuasive characters who disliked Paul and strove to undermine his authority.

It is not hard to understand how a smear campaign could be launched among the immature Corinthian Christians, still smarting from Paul's tough letter. Moreover, Paul had unwittingly played into his detractors' hands by announcing a change of itinerary. Some time previously he had told the Corinthians that because he was so fond of them he planned to visit them twice on his next tour of Greece; once on his way up to Macedonia, and again on his way back. Now, it seems, that plan had been abandoned. His rivals at Corinth were quick to exploit the sense of frustration and disappointment which the Corinthian church felt as a result. 'Ah, this Paul!' they said. 'He is not worth the high regard in which you hold him. He's deceitful. It's obvious he did not really mean it when he gave us all that flattery about coming to see us twice; it was just a ruse to butter us up. He's fickle too. He can't make up his mind. He is the sort of shifty fellow who is always saying one thing and doing another. You cannot rely on the man; he is inconsistent, he is frivolous.'

But for Paul, the unkindest cut of all was their accusation that he did not care about the Corinthians, that he was indifferent to them. 'He does not really like you at all,' they were saying. 'He is not bothered about you. If he were, he would have visited you as he promised. This nasty letter and this cancelled visit –they only go to prove the contempt in which he really holds you. You would be much better off to forget about Paul. After all, he is not a proper apostle, you know. He doesn't have the right papers or gifts. He's just a charlatan.'

As we saw in our last chapter, it was against this kind of background that 2 Corinthians was written: Paul uncharacteristically on the defensive, seeking to rebut the conspiracy of innuendo and allegation that had been organised against him. And in the passage we now turn to, you will see that he does so in three stages.

1. The charge of deceitfulness (1:12-14)

> Now this is our boast: Our conscience testifies that we have
> conducted ourselves in the world, and especially in our
> relations with you, in the holiness and sincerity that are from
> God. We have done so not according to worldly wisdom but
> according to God's grace (1:12).

Boasting, as we shall see several times in this book, was something
at which Paul's rivals seem to have excelled. But Paul found
boasting embarrassing. He did not like talking about himself at the
best of times, and to be forced into the position of having to blow his
own trumpet in order to vindicate himself against these unfair
allegations was unpalatable to him in the extreme.

Nevertheless, if boasting were necessary he was determined at
least to make sure that unlike his rivals he would boast about the
things a person *ought* to boast about. 'If there is one thing that I do
take some personal satisfaction from, it is this: that I have never used
deceit to further my ministry. Never. My conscience on this point is
utterly clear,' Paul says. 'And if you who knew me personally were
a little more honest yourselves, you would admit the fact. I have
maintained scrupulous fidelity to the truth in all my dealings with
everybody, and not least with you Corinthians. For if there is one
thing I value above everything else, it is my unsullied reputation for
holiness and sincerity.'

Holiness and sincerity, Paul claims, are not for him just a matter
of public image designed to impress. His is not the phoney sincerity
of the salesman or the contrived sincerity of the film star. There is no
human artifice in it. 'These qualities of holiness and sincerity come
from God. They are his, I take no credit for them at all,' he says. 'We
have done so not according to worldly wisdom, but according to
God's grace.'

This is one of the wonderful things about being a Christian. It
liberates us from the pretentiousness with which virtue is so often
associated. Paul can speak of the holiness and the sincerity of his life

and do so humbly, without a trace of the smugness or self-congratulation usually associated with such claims. He could do so because he was so transparently conscious of his indebtedness to God. 'This is not my doing; it is not worldly wisdom; it is God's grace.' Would that there were more goodness of that self-effacing, God-glorifying kind! It might help people to realise that you do not have to be sanctimonious in order to be saintly.

There is an ingenuousness about Paul's sincerity. It was his habit to speak frankly and straightforwardly, without a hint of artificiality or pseudo-sophistication, because he really did not need to try to pull the wool over anybody's eyes. He was quite happy for people to see him as the man he really was – a sinner, saved by grace. Only the experience of God's grace can give a person that kind of artless candour.

What is more, because of Paul's characteristic fundamental simplicity the Corinthians did not need to look for hidden meanings in his words.

> We do not write you anything you cannot read or understand. And I hope that, as you have understood us in part, you will come to understand fully... (1:13-14).

There is a double play on words here which it is impossible to render in the English translation. Firstly, the Greek words for 'to read' and 'to understand' both come from the same root, so they rhyme. Secondly, the verb 'to understand' has within its large range of meanings both the idea of recognising somebody as a result of having personally met them, and of giving somebody recognition as a mark of your personal esteem. When you put all that together you can see that what Paul is really implying, in a very compressed way, is something like this: 'You do not have to try to read between the lines of my letters' (some scholars would do well to note that!). 'There is no clever use of ambiguous phrases to conceal my real intentions, no *double-entendres*, no empty rhetoric like that with which those Greek orators love to embroider their speeches. No, I am the sort of person who says what he means and means what he says, and those of you who have known me in the past will corroborate this aspect of my character first-hand, and give me the recognition, the understanding that I deserve.'

Paul is of course very aware that it was just that recognition which the aspersions of his rivals called into doubt, hence his rather wistful 'I hope' in verse 13. 'Some of you at least have given me the recognition my honesty deserves ... I just hope this partial measure of support among you is not going to evaporate, so that on the last day we are going to be an embarrassment to one another. For when Jesus comes again, all the masks of deceit behind which men have concealed their true feelings and their true ambitions, are all going to be stripped away.'

Paul is sure that would leave the Corinthians blushing with shame at the suspicions they have so needlessly harboured. More, it would leave him blushing too, for what father is there who does not feel implicated in the humiliation of his children?

In this first paragraph, I suggest that there is a very salutary lesson about Christian integrity, and its importance. I suspect, terrible as it may seem to say it, that many of us do not speak to each other straight from the shoulder in the way Paul advocates here. Many of us habitually cloak our real thoughts in veils of equivocation and double-talk. If that lack of openness were due to the fear of hurting one another's feelings, it might be forgivable, but I fear that it usually has a great deal more to do with not wanting to dent our own image or forfeit people's respect for us. 'What will he think of me if I say that?' we say to ourselves. 'If I speak my mind, will she gossip it all round the church?'

So we play safe. We keep our problems, our doubts, our feelings to ourselves. We may call it being 'tactful' or 'discreet', but sometimes, sadly, it comes close to duplicity. We may make a great show of outward sincerity, and assure people that we really do mean what we say, but there is something rather unctuous and artificial about our sincerity, and consequently people do not really believe we will keep our word. Would it not be wonderful if we could all say with

Paul: 'This is my boast: I conduct myself in the world at large, and especially in the church, in the holiness and sincerity that comes from God. I keep nothing up my sleeve; my word accurately mirrors my thought: I say what I mean, and I mean what I say'?

Jesus, in the Sermon on the Mount, said that that is precisely the sort of thing he expected of Christian character (Matthew 5:37).

2. The charge of fickleness (1:15-22)

> **Because I was confident of this, I planned to visit you first so that you might benefit twice. I planned to visit you on my way to Macedonia and to come back to you from Macedonia, and then to have you send me on my way to Judea. When I planned this, did I do it lightly? Or do I make my plans in a worldly manner so that in the same breath I say, "Yes, yes", and "No, no"? (1:15-17).**

There are some Christians who seem to expect every step they take to be infallibly communicated to them by supernatural directives from on high. They are the ones who are always looking for 'signs'. The tiniest event has to mean something – a car number-plate ahead of them on the motor way, a misdirected letter in the post, a chance meeting on the street – every incident in their life is regarded as a kind of code that they must decipher in order to determine God's will for them. Or there are those who are always looking for 'messages', spiritual hunches that suddenly pop into their minds, or dreams, or prophetic words from other Christians. Such people end up regarding themselves as a kind of spiritual robot, obeying explicit instructions from the heavenly programmer! Jim Packer recounts the true story of a woman who would never get up in the morning unless she 'felt led', and would sit on the side of her bed for minutes on end waiting for a similar prompting before she would put on her stockings.

Paul's words here are immensely valuable because they debunk that whole super-spiritual attitude towards Christian guidance. Please do not misunderstand me; I am not suggesting that God does not sometimes direct Christians by special providences or events. Neither am I denying that the Holy Spirit does sometimes burden our hearts with a particular matter, or give intuitive insights to somebody else on our behalf. All Christians know that these things sometimes happen. But none of this constitutes the normal mode of guidance for a Christian, any more than Paul's famous nocturnal vision of a man of Macedonia was the normal way that he decided his next port of call. Notice the phrase that Paul uses repeatedly in these verses? 'I planned'. He does not feel obliged to use pious clichés like 'I felt led' or 'The Lord told me'. Here we have a rational man, making rational decisions. Clearly he did not feel it was presumptuous for a Christian to do so, nor that he should wait before making any decisions until some mysterious providence, inner prompting or prophetic message told him what to do. He *planned*. In fact, the expression he uses in 2:1 makes the point even more clearly: 'I made up my mind' - literally, 'I judged for myself'. Apostle that he was, even Paul did not get his guidance down some mystical drainpipe from heaven!

He received his apostolic teaching by divine revelation, it's true. He is very definite about that. But there was nothing similarly supernatural and infallible about his personal decision-making. Sometimes, he made plans and had to change them. Sometimes he made decisions and had to go back on them, as all human beings do. And the visit to Corinth was a case in point. He had made up his mind, and then he had changed his mind.

'Does that make me unspiritual?' he asks. 'Am I a fickle, vacillating, worldly man who is always oscillating between saying "Yes" and "No" as the fancy takes him? Because I changed my mind about this visit?'

Clearly, Paul felt there were no grounds for such an impeachment. And that in itself is an important lesson to us. If I may speak frankly to you (as Paul seems to be encouraging in verse 12), I become nervous when people make too much use of the phrase 'the Lord told me'. I may be doing them an injustice – I probably am, in some cases – but I suspect that many people who speak in that way are in fact deceiving themselves out of a subconscious desire to escape responsibility for their own lives. It is a terribly convenient thing to say 'The Lord told me.' It means that no-one can contradict you, and no-one can ever accuse you of having made a mistake. Whatever happens, you never have to say, 'I was wrong,' because even if the action is utterly irresponsible and has horrendous consequences, it must all be the Lord's will because, after all, 'He told me'!

But Paul feels no need to rationalise his private judgments in that way. 'I planned,' he said, 'and I changed my plan. No special guidance led me to the former or the latter' – but then, no special guidance led Paul to the vast majority of the decisions he took, and no special guidance will lead us to the vast majority of the decisions we take.

Paul did not see himself as a robot whose every action must be specifically commanded by remote control. He was a Christian human being, and a human being has self-determination. That is what distinguishes a human from a robot. As human beings we are responsible to God for the use we make of our power of choice and our ability to plan. To accuse Paul of fickleness was to reveal a complete misunderstanding of the nature of Christian spirituality; one might say, of Christian humanity.

But then, judging from the evidence later on in this letter, it is likely that these rivals of Paul at Corinth did misunderstand Christian spirituality in that way. Almost certainly, to judge from later chapters, they were deeply involved in mystical experiences of one kind or another. In their view, a really holy man had to be surrounded by a permanent aura of the supernatural. That was one of the things they believed was wrong with Paul. He was far too ordinary, far too human. A real apostle would not have to change his plans, he would get his plans through a direct satellite link with heaven. But in Paul's judgment that was simply not the case. To pretend that it was, and to accuse him of unspiritual fickleness because he refused to conform to that false model of Christian guidance, was not only unfair, Paul argued; it was also thoroughly mischievous.

> **But as surely as God is faithful, our message to you is not
> "Yes" and "No"** (1:18).

Here we begin to see why Paul's integrity was so important to him.
It was not just a question of defending his personal reputation; he
was quite prepared to be slandered, as he had been on numerous
occasions. But this particular slander had an unacceptable corollary,
so far as Paul was concerned. Any impeachment of his trustworthiness inevitably placed a question-mark against the trustworthiness
of his message, the gospel. And that was a conclusion that he could
not allow to pass unchallenged. That is why his reputation for
honesty was so important to him. They could call him a fool and he
would not bother about that, but he was not prepared to have
anybody call him a liar.

> **For the Son of God, Jesus Christ, who was preached among
> you by me and Silas and Timothy, was not "Yes" and "No",
> but in him it has always been "Yes". For no matter how
> many promises God has made, they are "Yes" in Christ.
> And so through him the "Amen" is spoken by us to the glory
> of God** (1:19-20).

The Jesus whom Paul preaches is utterly reliable. There is no
fickleness about him. Jesus does not represent a change of plan on
God's part, but an emphatic endorsement of God's plans. Everything that he ever said in the Old Testament is confirmed by the
incontrovertible affirmative of Jesus. He is the 'yes' to all God's
promises. That is why we Christians are called upon not to question
God's purposes, but to pronounce our 'Amen' in acknowledgment
of their successful accomplishment. 'That is why,' says Paul, 'when
I preach I offer no dialectical approach such as the Greek philosophers did – look at things this way and look at things that way, as if
the truth would simply emerge out of the contradictions of human
debate – I proclaim Jesus, the Son of God, the unequivocal solution
to all men's spiritual searchings.' And, he says, if you want to know
how I can be so sure of Jesus in this way, I give it as my testimony
that God has made me sure:

> Now it is God who makes both us and you stand firm in
> Christ. He anointed us, set his seal of ownership on us, and
> put his Spirit in our hearts as a deposit, guaranteeing what
> is to come (1:21-22).

It was the work of God's Spirit to plant this confidence about Jesus in Paul's heart and mind.

Paul uses three metaphors from the law of contract to drive home the unshakeable nature of his Christian convictions: 'We stand firm in Christ' – a word which meant 'to make legally binding', as when signing an agreement; 'He set his seal upon us' – an act, again, which was performed in a legal context to confirm the authenticity of a document; and 'guaranteeing what is to come' – a word that describes the deposit made to make a contract of sale certain.

All these metaphors speak of the way in which the Spirit of God has made Paul not just a vehicle of God's promises, but a living demonstration of their trustworthiness. Paul's reliability was absolutely vital for the presentation of the gospel. With a boldness that comes close to scandalous, he says, 'God has even anointed us as he anointed Jesus the Christ. So to call me, the apostle Paul, or my colleagues Silas and Timothy, unreliable is not just a slur on our Christian character, it is to impugn the credibility of the gospel I preach. When you question the reliability of an apostle's words, you challenge the reliability of the word of God himself.'

That was how he felt about it. He wanted the Corinthians to realise the seriousness of the charge of fickleness, and his utter determination to repudiate it.

But there was a third and more personal reason for his concern about these accusations, too.

3. The charge of emotional indifference (1:23-2:11)

> I call God as my witness that it was in order to spare you that
> I did not return to Corinth. Not that we lord it over your
> faith, but we work with you for your joy, because it is by faith
> you stand firm. So I made up my mind that I would not

> make another painful visit to you. For if I grieve you, who
> is left to make me glad but you whom I have grieved? I wrote
> as I did so that when I came I should not be distressed by
> those who ought to make me rejoice. I had confidence in all
> of you, that you would all share my joy. For I wrote you out
> of great distress and anguish of heart and with many tears,
> not to grieve you but to let you know the depth of my love for
> you (1:23-2:4).

Those of you who are in business will know that practically any
modern factory will have a department in it labelled 'Quality
Control'. A good businessman knows that the reputation of his firm
depends upon the reliability of his products, and he will want to be
sure that nothing inferior or mediocre escapes the factory.

The Bible tells us that the Lord demonstrates a similar concern
for his church. He is not just interested in her numerical increase; he
is interested in the quality and calibre of her membership. He
practises quality control too. There are some very important words
on this matter in the Gospel of Matthew, from the mouth of Jesus
himself:

> If your brother sins against you, go and show him his fault, just
> between the two of you. If he listens to you, you have won your
> brother over. But if he will not listen, take one or two [other
> Christians] along, so that 'every matter may be established by
> the testimony of two or three witnesses'. If he refuses to listen
> to them, tell it to the church; and if he refuses to listen even to
> the church, treat him as you would a pagan [in other words,
> excommunicate him] (Matthew 18:15-17).

The passage we are studying in this chapter is set against the
background of just such an incident of church discipline, and now
it begins to come to the surface. Scholars differ about what precisely
the offence in question was. Some, adopting the more traditional
line of interpretation, think that the offender in question was identical with the man Paul mentions in his first letter to the Corinthians,
who was guilty of serious sexual immorality (see 1 Corinthians 5).

More recent scholars, on the basis of internal evidence in 2 Corinthians, tend to feel that the issue must have been a personal slight against the apostle himself or one of his representatives like Timothy.

For our purposes it does not really matter which of the two is correct; you can find the arguments for both sides in any good commentary if you are interested. We need simply note that what Paul is saying is that the harsh letter and the cancelled visit which had both caused so much ill-feeling were bound up with this case of church discipline, which the Corinthians knew all about.

The severe letter, for example, was written because Paul felt he had to insist that this disciplinary matter be dealt with firmly in Corinth. To suggest that he composed it in a spirit of callous or autocratic contempt for the feelings of the Corinthian congregation was simply untrue. On the contrary, he wrote in a state of great distress; his heart was broken, his eyes filled with tears even as his pen scratched the paper. 'I did not enjoy hurting you,' Paul says. 'It was precisely because my love for you was so deep, that I felt I just had to write it. It hurt me more than it hurt you.'

As for the cancelled visit, the cancellation was simply because he could not face the emotional trauma of more ugly scenes, and he knew ugly scenes were bound to result if he came among them while the disciplinary matter was still unresolved. 'You see, I have so many happy memories of you Corinthians, I did not want them spoiled. I was sure that the cloud that had fallen between us would be just a passing shadow, that you would respond to my letter and put the matter right. And that is why I decided to wait till the disciplinary case had been settled before I returned to you, so that when I did come, my visit would be unmarred by bad feeling.'

Why, he says in verse 3, he had made that very point in the letter itself (for that is the force of the Greek); do they not remember? So how can they accuse him of indifference? It was because he loved them that he sent them that harsh letter. It was because he loved them that he spared them a severe visit. 'I do not like playing the role of spiritual heavyweight, of lording it over you. That is not the kind of relationship I want with you. I only want to be your friend, working with you for your joy – not some resented, ecclesiastical despot. That is why I stayed away. I wanted to give you the opportunity to handle the problem on your own. Can't you see that far from expressing my indifference, these things have happened only to confirm the depth of my love for you all?' It is a classic case of 'This has hurt me more than it has hurt you.'

If you look on to Chapter 7, you will find Paul takes up the subject of this disciplinary action again. It is clear from what he writes there that his tears were not in vain. The harsh letter he wrote was heeded. The erring church member was disciplined. That is why Paul can go on here in Chapter 2 as he does.

> **The punishment inflicted on him by the majority is suffi-
> cient for him. Now instead, you ought to forgive and comfort
> him, so that he will not be overwhelmed by excessive sorrow.
> I urge you, therefore, to reaffirm your love for him** (2:6-8).

Probably 'punishment' should be rendered 'public rebuke'. And I am fairly sure that the call to 'reaffirm your love for him' similarly implies some kind of public act of reconciliation. The Greek word used has decidedly legal overtones. You could almost translate it, 'ratify' your love for him. Certainly there is no shortage of New Testament passages to confirm that the early church did discipline its membership in this kind of formal way, with public rebukes and public reconciliations. Like a modern football referee, Paul called upon them to give this man an official warning, and they did. He had been banned from a few matches. And the treatment had worked: he was plainly repentant now. It was time, said Paul, to reinstate him in the team –'reaffirm your love for him'.

This pattern of rebuke and restoration is rare to the point of extinction in the vast majority of churches today. That is why I have had to explain it – because it is so foreign to most of us. The reason it is such a foreign idea of course is because that kind of discipline seems to us in the twentieth century to be rather uncharitable and intolerant. It brings us back full-circle to where we began, with the question of corporal punishment. Paul's example in writing his severe letter and that of the Corinthian church in disciplining their erring member make it plain to us: love does hurt. And I have to say that if I regret the weakening of discipline in the home because of the sentimentality of our age, even more do I regret the weakening of discipline in the church, which has arisen from the same cause.

4. Lessons about church discipline
Let me list then some of the lessons we learn about church discipline in these verses.

(a) Sin within the membership injures the whole church

> If anyone has caused grief, he has not so much grieved me as he has grieved all of you, to some extent (2:5).

The church is not merely a collection of individuals; it is a body with a corporate identity. The sin of one member shames the whole; the hurt of one member hurts the whole. Whatever the particular offence in question was, the damage it had caused could not possibly be contained in the private life of the individual concerned; the church had to be involved in sorting it out, because the church's inner life was implicated in the affair.

Church discipline is the vital way in which the sense that we belong to one another is given meaning. We can no more be careless about the behaviour of other church members than we can be careless about members of our own family.

(b) Disciplinary action is to be taken by the church

> The punishment inflicted on him by the majority is sufficient for him (2:6).

It may be that the word 'majority' indicates that there was a lack of unanimity. Whether or not that is so, it is clear that the church took the action as a collective body. The church elders at Corinth, assuming there were such, could recommend it, but there was no way they could enforce it. Jesus makes that plain in that famous passage in Matthew that we have already referred to. Tell it to the church, he says: it is in the church that the power to discipline is invested.

How much more our church membership would mean to us if we realised that it involved participation in this kind of mutual care and mutual discipline, rather than simply joining a club, like the cricket or the photography club!

(c) The practice of discipline in the church is a necessary mark of the church

The reason I wrote you was to see if you would stand the test and be obedient in everything (2:9).

At the time of the Reformation, one of the things that distinguished the Anabaptists from the Reformers was their insistence that a true gospel church, in addition to being a church where the gospel was preached and the sacraments administered, must be a church marked by discipline. The church should not tolerate heresy or sin among its members, the Anabaptists said; when such error or sin occurred, the church should respond just as Matthew 18 laid down, by public rebuke or if necessary, by excommunication. This was not just a desirable feature of church life; it was, they insisted, a necessary feature by which a true church could be distinguished from an apostate church.

It appears that Paul would have had sympathy with that strong line. For him, the test of whether the Corinthian church was willing to grasp the prickly nettle of dealing with a disciplined offender was an index of the spirituality of the church.

Of course it is very easy for us to rationalise or sentimentalise our way out of church discipline. 'Oh,' we can say, 'it is not really our business. I am not qualified to interfere. Jesus tells us not to judge one another – least said, soonest mended. Surely we must be tolerant these days' – and so on. No doubt there was a 'Let's do nothing about it' lobby in Corinth, too. But as far as Paul was concerned, he had written that difficult letter spelling the issue out so precisely, because in his mind it was a test case. Were the Corinthians a club that wrote their own constitution – or were they an apostolic church that submitted to the revealed word of God in all their faith and conduct? The issue of discipline is not left open in the Bible, it is clearly put. And the congregation that through embarrassment, fear or cultural conditioning refuses to practise discipline is in grave danger of forfeiting their status as an apostolic church, just as Corinth would have been had she not responded the way she did to Paul's letter.

(d) Church discipline is always intended to be remedial

Now instead, you ought to forgive and comfort him, so that he will not be overwhelmed by excessive sorrow (2:7).

Final judgment does not lie in the power of the church. The power that Christ has bestowed upon the local church is one of chastening only. For that reason, it must always aim at the restoration of the offender. Forgive, says Paul. Show grace to him, comfort him. Literally, 'get alongside and encourage him' – because if you don't, says Paul, he may be drowned by despair.

In a fellowship as close as a church ought to be, the act of suspension or excommunication could bring immense emotional and social deprivation to a person. It is a terrible thing to feel that one does not belong any more. And it is an indication of the superficiality of our corporate Christian consciousness if we can contemplate being separated from Christian fellowship with no such agony or spiritual homesickness. 'You must not let this brother suffer indefinitely,' says Paul; 'the mere fact that he feels so grief-stricken about your verdict proves that he really is a child of God. If he were not, he would not care so much.

'As it is, he is a spiritual refugee now, a misplaced person; he is alienated from the world, and he is alienated from the church. And to allow him to remain in such a state of spiritual limbo for long is to risk reducing him to utter despair. It is time to reach out to him and reassure him of his acceptance among you,' says Paul; 'he has suffered enough, he has learned his lesson. Reaffirm your love for him, because otherwise the cure could turn out to be more disastrous than the disease.'

(e) Church discipline can be exploited by the devil for his purposes

What I have forgiven - if there was anything to forgive - I have forgiven in the sight of Christ for your sake, in order that Satan might not outwit us. For we are not unaware of his schemes (2:10-11).

Some Christian groups have practised discipline with such severity that marriages have been broken, children have been alienated from parents, and even minds have been deranged. Some have taught a doctrine of 'shepherding' which when taken to excess can lead to elders playing God to believers under their charge and requiring a type of allegiance that squashes all personal responsibility and instils a slavish fear and sense of dependence.

On many occasions Satan has perverted a laudable ambition for the purity of the church into a sordid witch-hunt or persecuting inquisition or authoritarian tyranny. That is why Paul talks about him 'outwitting' us. The verb actually contains the idea of defrauding somebody by seizing more than one's due. I suspect that Paul is thinking there of the way that a reckless and relentless use of church discipline can actually have the effect of putting those who should be safe in the family of God into the domain of Satan, where they have no right to be because they do not belong to him. Chrysostom comments on this passage:

To take men by sin is Satan's proper work. For Satan to take men by the discouragements of an excessive sorrow for sin is far more than Satan's due. Repentance is our weapon not his.

How we must beware, then, of a spirit of harshness in this matter of discipline! Discipline is necessary, for sin injures the church and we cannot be indifferent to it. The church has a responsibility to discipline its members, laid upon it by apostolic command, but that discipline must be remedial and forgiving in its goal. If not, Satan will turn it against us, and make of us a hellish jungle of uncharitable recriminations and puritanical petty-mindedness.

Surely the safety check lies in that proverb with which we began. 'This is going to hurt me more than it hurts you.' Loving discipline will always be reluctant discipline.

Some people derive a self-righteous satisfaction from pronouncing apocalyptic censures upon the errors and sins of others. The judgements they pronounce are not necessarily wrong, but they enjoy it all far too much. We are not going to be able to make others weep for that which we have never wept. Love hurts. It hurts because it needs to, sometimes. But when it needs to, it feels hurt itself in return.

When you think about it, we Christians, of all the people in the world, ought to be in no doubt about that. For we have seen the cross; we have seen the Judge suffering out of love for the sinner. We, then, ought to know – even if the sentimentality of our age has forgotten it–how much love hurts.

3

The Lifted Veil
(2 Corinthians 2:12-3:18)

Now when I went to Troas to preach the gospel of Christ and found that the Lord had opened a door for me, I still had no peace of mind, because I did not find my brother Titus there. So I said good-bye to them and went on to Macedonia.

But thanks be to God, who always leads us in triumphal procession in Christ and through us spreads everywhere the fragrance of the knowledge of him. For we are to God the aroma of Christ among those who are being saved and those who are perishing. To the one we are the smell of death; to the other, the fragrance of life. And who is equal to such a task? Unlike so many, we do not peddle the word of God for profit. On the contrary, in Christ we speak before God with sincerity, like men sent from God.

Are we beginning to commend ourselves again? Or do we need, like some people, letters of recommendation to you or from you? You yourselves are our letter, written on our hearts, known and read by everybody. You show that you are a letter from Christ, the result of our ministry, written not with ink but with the Spirit of the living God, not on tablets of stone but on tablets of human hearts.

Such confidence as this is ours through Christ before God. Not that we are competent in ourselves to claim anything for ourselves, but our competence comes from God. He has made us competent as ministers of a new covenant –not of the letter but of the Spirit; for the letter kills, but the Spirit gives life.

Now if the ministry that brought death, which was engraved in letters on stone, came with glory, so that the Israelites could not look steadily at the face of Moses because of its glory, fading though it was, will not the ministry of the Spirit be even more glorious? If the ministry that condemns men is glorious, how much more glorious is the ministry that brings righteousness! For what was glorious has no glory now in comparison with the surpassing glory. And if what was fading away came with glory, how much greater is the glory of that which lasts!

Therefore, since we have such a hope, we are very bold. We are not like Moses, who would put a veil over his face to keep the Israelites from gazing at it while the radiance was fading away. But their minds were made dull, for to this day the same veil remains when the old covenant is read. It has not been removed, because only in Christ is it taken away. Even to this day when Moses is read, a veil covers their hearts. But whenever anyone turns to the Lord, the veil is taken away. Now the Lord is the Spirit, and where the Spirit of the Lord is, there is freedom. And we, who with unveiled faces all reflect the Lord's glory, are being transformed into his likeness with ever-increasing glory, which comes from the Lord, who is the Spirit (2 Corinthians 2:12-3:18).

CAN YOU KEEP A SECRET?

It's amazing how that question never fails to grab people's attention. Immediately, our ears prick up; whether it is a furtive whisper behind a cupped hand in a school playground, or a confidential government paper leaked to a newspaper reporter with a knowing wink. We all love secrets. There is a special kind of thrill associated with knowing something that nobody else does. It is hardly surprising that often, throughout history, religions have exploited that thrill. Technically they are called 'esoteric' religions: religions that are designed for an exclusive circle of initiated disciples, religions built around the question, 'Can you keep a secret?'

There are countless examples, from theosophical societies to witches' covens, from the Druse people of the Middle East to the Freemasons of the City of London. The hallmarks are always the same: clandestine gatherings, cabalistic signs, arcane rituals, dark mysteries. These are the stuff of which secret sects and cults are made the world over.

And of course the church has not been immune to such influences. Usually on the margins of orthodoxy, often slipping over the boundary into heresy, there have been many examples of esoteric Christianity, Christianity that wants to keep secrets. The phenomenon began very soon after the church was born. It might be argued, indeed, that there are things in the Bible that rather invite such a development. The parables, for instance. Jesus said to the Twelve:

> The knowledge of the secrets of the kingdom of God has been given to you, but to others I speak in parables, so that, 'though seeing, they may not see; though hearing, they may not understand' (Luke 8:10).

So is not a parable a kind of cryptogram, designed to keep secret the spiritual insight that Jesus brought? The sacraments of baptism and communion, too: are they not classic examples of the kind of hocus-pocus with which secret societies seek to veil their activities in mystery? It is certainly not hard to see how such traditions and rites within the church could be exploited by those interested in the esoteric dimension of religion.

And it is important to recognise that there were plenty of people around in the first century who were so interested. Among the Greeks, for instance, the mystery cults were enormously popular. The Greek word 'mystery' means a secret. The cults were very typical of the kind of esoteric religion we are talking about, with their initiation ceremonies and claims to unique mystical experiences which only their initiates could share. Among the Jews too, esotericism was quite well known in the first century. There were apocalyptic groups, for instance, that developed their own codes using secret symbols and numbers, and there were monastic societies like the Qumran community that had special rituals and teaching that only their disciples could understand.

But the most obvious evidence of the popularity of this kind of 'can you keep a secret' religion in first-century culture was the popular obsession with magic, among both the Jews and the Greeks. Magic, with its spells and potions, is a classic example of esoteric religion. The very word 'occult' means 'hidden'. And in the world of the New Testament, occultism was close to being a part of everyday life. There were countless wizards and exorcists and soothsayers and mediums, making a living out of their claims to possess supernatural powers of one kind or another.

In such an environment it is not surprising that the church was vulnerable to the infiltration of esoteric ideas. In fact, we know that in the second century, a major heresy of precisely this type was threatening the early church. It was generally called 'gnosticism', and it treated Christianity as if it were a mystery religion, offering secret knowledge or *gnosis* to those lucky enough to be initiated into it.

The reason I have described esoteric religion at such length is that I think it may help us to understand 2 Corinthians, and particularly that part of it we shall be considering in this and the next chapter.

Many scholars have complained that 2 Corinthians 2:12-3:18 seems to lack any clear logical order. You can see the problem even in translation: Paul seems to break off at the end of verse 13 from telling us about his visit to Macedonia, and to embark on an unexpected doxology. Then in Chapter 3 he goes off at a tangent again into a long discourse about the old covenant. It is not until 7:5 that he at last returns to finish telling us about Macedonia.

One explanation that is often offered is that 2 Corinthians, as we have it, is in fact several letters stuck together like a composite motion at a political party conference. In such a flow of thought there are inevitably a few dislocations of logic.

But as I read this passage, it seems to me that there is no need to invoke dislocations or even undisciplined digressions to explain why Paul speaks as he does at this point. A recurring theme can be identified that resides at the back of the apostle's mind and which integrates the whole section, even though he does pursue a rather circuitous route at times. That theme is the openness, the candour, the exoteric character of the Christian gospel.

The key verse perhaps is 3:12. 'Since we have such a hope, we are very bold' or, as it could equally well be translated: 'We employ great outspokenness'. That Greek word for 'bold' has a rich background. In political context, it meant the democratic right of free speech. By extension, in popular usage it came to mean any kind of courageous and undisguised self-expression. Paul is at great pains in this section of his letter to affirm that such a frankness and honesty was characteristic of his ministry. 'We use great boldness, great outspokenness,' he says. Or, as he continues in 4:2, 'We have renounced secret, shameful ways. We set forth the truth plainly.'

But why should Paul feel it necessary to emphasise this? I suspect the most likely explanation is that there were in Corinth some who did not approve of such a policy of promiscuous and unreserved exposure in matters of the Christian faith. As we have already seen, one of Paul's main reasons for writing this letter is that he was under personal attack from a group of would-be leaders who had infiltrated the Corinthian church since his departure. All we know of their identity has to be deduced from the internal evidence of the letter itself. However, there is a very strong likelihood that they represented a rather esoteric understanding of Christianity. It is certain that they were keen on secret revelations and supernatural power: we know that from what Paul says later on. It is also certain that, rather like the magicians of those days, they charged fees for their professional services.

Maybe they were heirs of Simon Magus, divines who were seeking to fuse Christianity with the professional magic circle of the first century. Or maybe they had been influenced by Jewish apocalyptic groups and secret sects – they were certainly Jews. Or were they precursors of the Gnostics who were to trouble the church in later years? Certainly Paul's first letter to the Corinthians strongly suggests the presence of some such incipient heresy in the church.

We cannot be sure who they were. But what is plain, to judge by Paul's defensiveness on the subject, is that the openness of Paul's Christian preaching was offensive to them, and they were using their criticism of his missionary style as fuel in their campaign to undermine his authority. Perhaps they argued something like this: 'Religious mysteries should not be prostituted among the general public. Such holy secrets should be kept private within the church until people are properly initiated and have paid the proper fee for membership, and so forth.'

I believe this background serves as a key to unlock the rather disjointed section of Paul's letter that we have come to. I am certain that one of the things that Paul wanted to stress throughout these chapters is that there was nothing secret or esoteric about his religion. His was a religion that demanded candour. The gospel rightly belongs to the public domain.

1. A man whose life made a public impact (2:12–3:5)

> Now when I went to Troas to preach the gospel of Christ and found that the Lord had opened a door for me, I still had no peace of mind, because I did not find my brother Titus there. So I said good-bye to them and went on to Macedonia. But thanks be to God, who always leads us in triumphal procession in Christ and through us spreads everywhere the fragrance of the knowledge of him (2:12–14).

It seems from these verses that Paul had a speaking engagement at Troas but was clearly not in the mood for preaching. Later, in Chapter 7, he speaks of sleepless nights and disturbed thoughts.

The reason for this restlessness, as the earlier verses in chapter 2 make plain, is that he was deeply concerned about the situation at Corinth. The church there was one in which he had invested a great deal of time. Being a major urban centre it was particularly strategic for Paul, but he had heard about the anti-Pauline faction that had invaded the congregation and was profoundly worried about the damage they might be doing. He sent his colleague Titus to try and sort things out, but he was late returning and the more the days slipped by on the calendar, the more anxious did Paul become. Eventually, he tells us, he was so frustrated that he decided to leave Troas prematurely and take a ship to Macedonia in the hope of meeting Titus earlier.

It is an indication of just how upset and worried the apostle was that he could abandon the opening that was developing in Troas. 'The Lord had opened a door for me,' he says. But it was a door he was prepared to walk away from, so preoccupied was he with the fate of Corinth. It is interesting that in spite of the fact that Paul did not want to continue his missionary work at that particular moment, it seems that evangelistic success followed him nevertheless wherever he went – that seems to be the implication of verse 14:

> **But thanks be to God, who always leads us in triumphal procession in Christ and through us spreads everywhere the fragrance of the knowledge of him.**

It is a particularly graphic metaphor. 'Triumphal procession' speaks of a victory carnival such as a Roman general might lead following a successful military campaign. There would be two sorts of people following in such a procession. On one hand there would be the troops who had won the battle and would therefore share the commander's honour. On the other hand, there would be the prisoners of war captured in the battle who would be exposed to ridicule and disgrace as part of the general celebration.

It is debatable to which of those two companies Paul imagines himself belonging. Undoubtedly, he was a 'good soldier' of Jesus Christ, but he often speaks of himself too as the 'prisoner of Christ'. When in 1 Corinthians 4 he used this metaphor once before, it was with the latter thought in mind. 'We apostles,' he says, 'we are used to being mocked, because we are like gladiators, put on display in God's procession, before being condemned to die in the arena.' It is not clear whether verse 14 here has that same ironic edge. But whether it has or not, the general thrust of what he is saying is clear: 'I am part of a parade. There can be no secret, then, about my gospel. Whether I like it or not, even when I am not feeling like it, every-where I go I am on open exhibition, I am an advertisement for Christ. Whether men honour me as one of God's lieutenants or mock me as one of his clowns, I am part of God's triumphal march through the world. I am a trophy of his conquest and an instrument of his victory.'

That kind of public impact, he says, is something he has not sought; it has sought him. God just seems graciously to use him even when, as in Troas, his mind is on other things. It is, he assures them, quite a responsibility:

> For we are to God the aroma of Christ among those who are being saved and those who are perishing. To the one we are the smell of death; to the other, the fragrance of life. And who is equal to such a task? (2:15-16)

There is a touch of genius here as Paul switches his metaphor. No longer is he a soldier or slave in the triumphal procession; now he is the burning incense that was always carried along as part of the carnival. Yet once again the underlying implication is that Paul's impact is a universal, public one. He just cannot prevent it being so. 'Christian or non-Christian,' he says, 'I influence them all.' To the one an alluring perfume, a spiritual oxygen that breathes life into their souls; to the other a stench in their nostrils, a spiritual cyanide that suffocates and poisons them to death. But neither have any doubt about his presence; neither can meet him and go away unaffected. 'For my gospel is like that; you cannot keep it secret, any more than you can prevent the diffusion of gas through the atmosphere. Through God we spread the fragrance of Christ everywhere.'

In verse 14 that little word 'knowledge' is, in the Greek, *gnosis*. In the light of the later gnostic movement, that could be significant. It is clear from verse 17 that Paul is consciously reacting against a very different style of preacher whom they in Corinth knew all about.

> **Unlike so many, we do not peddle the word of God for profit. On the contrary, in Christ we speak before God with sincerity, like men sent from God (2:17).**

'Oh yes,' says Paul, 'there may be some so-called preachers who talk a lot about knowledge but are less overt and forthright than me as far as declaring what that 'knowledge' is. If so, they expose themselves as not being true apostles of the word at all, but mere peddlers of it.'

The word 'peddler' has two associations in Greek: the peddler was first of all someone who traded for profit in a rather dubious way – a huckster, always on the fiddle, like Del Boy in television's *Only Fools and Horses*. If that was the connotation uppermost in Paul's mind he is saying: 'Look, the reason these people want to be secretive about the gospel is because they have a financial interest in doing so. What gypsy tells your fortune before you have crossed his palm with silver? What magician reveals his spells until you have paid the appropriate fee? Don't you see, these esoteric Christians, they are just sharks, they are not men of God at all!'

The other popular association of the word 'peddler' was that of adulterating goods in order to surreptitiously increase the profit margin. Peddlers were people who watered down their wine, or mixed chalk with their salt. And if that is the association in Paul's mind here, then he is saying, 'Look, the only reason these people can even suggest that the gospel should be put on restricted access to the general public is because they have diluted its message. If they realised what a life-and-death issue people's response to Jesus Christ was, they could no more charge fees for telling people about him than a doctor could charge fees for attending at a major road accident.'

Either way, whether it is as profiteers or adulterators or both, those who keep the gospel in wraps – the wraps of an esoteric cult – they are not authentic apostles. 'True apostles,' says Paul, 'do not take our model from the professional occultists or the mystery-religion priests who ply their trade around the world. No, we are in the tradition of the prophets who spoke the word of God with utter integrity and with no thought of personal gain. We speak as men sent from God, never ashamed to be those whose lives make a public impact.'

There are many lessons to learn in what Paul is saying here.

There is a lesson for *preachers*: 'Unlike *so many* we do not peddle the word of God for profit' – that is a disturbing statistic. Paul feels authentic preachers are in the minority. Could it still be so today? Are there still more hucksters and corrupters of God's word in the world than there are genuine proclaimers of the truth?

There is a word too for *non-Christians*: 'To the one we are the smell of death; to the other, the fragrance of life.' There are only two stark alternatives. What a momentous thing it is, then, to hear the word of God! You must never come to church expecting entertainment. When we sit in front of a pulpit we place ourselves in a spiritual gas-chamber, either to receive God's grace, or his judgment.

But perhaps supremely, there is a lesson here for all who are *Christians*. According to Paul, it is a very serious thing to be a Christian. For we are potentially instruments of life and death to those around us. No wonder Paul asks who is equal to such a task! The responsibility that lies upon those of us who know Christ is to have the right kind of influence, to permeate the right kind of fragrance into the environment, to refuse to dilute the message or to run away from its life and death consequences.

If it is not too personal a question to ask – Christian, do you smell? You ought to, even at the risk of being an offensive stench in the nostrils of some. To be a Christian is to make a public impact, favourable or unfavourable, welcome or unwelcome. Do not smother yourself in spiritual deodorant. You are supposed to smell. You are supposed to reek of Jesus.

To give them their due, Paul seems to feel that the Corinthian church did.

> **Are we beginning to commend ourselves again? Or do we need, like some people, letters of recommendation to you or from you? You yourselves are our letter, written on our hearts, known and read by everybody. You show that you are a letter from Christ, the result of our ministry, written not with ink but with the Spirit of the living God, not on tablets of stone but on tablets of human hearts (3:1-3).**

It seems that in the early church travelling preachers often took references, letters of accreditation, when they went from one church to another. And to judge from Paul's sly comment 'like some people' in verse 1, his rivals in Corinth possessed such letters. Paul, however, as an apostle whose vocation proceeded direct from the risen Christ, had none. And this was being used against him. He refuses to be intimidated, however. He has a superior testimony to any of them – the Corinthian church itself. 'You are my reference,' says Paul. 'This is no confidential memo, it is an open confirmation of the power of the gospel. They talk of esoteric religion – how can Christianity keep itself secret, when its results in peoples' lives are so glaringly obvious? The church is no masonic lodge whose members can mingle anonymously with men, recognised by none but themselves. No, they are a piece of heavenly graffiti, placarded quite intentionally in the most public of places so that absolutely no-one can miss them.'

How transparent is our Christian testimony?

Somebody has asked, 'If Christianity were a crime, would there be enough evidence to convict you?' Paul's argument here suggests an adaptation of the question that might be addressed to preachers:

Suppose being a Christian preacher was made illegal – would there be enough evidence in the lives of your congregation to convict you? It is a searching thought for everybody who aspires to public ministry of God's word. Paul said his credentials were public property; anybody who looked at his congregation, anybody who looked into the lives of his converts, knew that he was a real apostle and not a charlatan.

But Paul's words challenge us as Christians whether or not we have pretensions to the ministry. The real authentication of the work of the Spirit in our lives, he says, is the testimony of our lives. When we stand before God on the last day he is not going to ask us for our baptismal certificate or a letter from our church elders saying that we came to church every Sunday. He is not even going to need a receipt from the church treasury to prove we paid our dues. Still less is he going to ask us for some secret password or handshake to prove we belong to the Christian lodge! If we are Christians, it will be obvious to everyone. Our credentials will be inscribed in the evidence of our own character. God will not need to look up our names in some membership book. Our lives will be an open book; they will tell him all he needs to know.

People sometimes talk about the possibility of being a secret Christian and cite the example of Joseph of Arimathea. But as far as I can see, the phenomenon of secret Christianity ended on the day of Pentecost. Once the Spirit came there could be no more hiding. He stamped the signature of Christ as if with indelible ink on every life he touched. That is why Peter told them to be baptised – publicly baptised. No secret initiation this; they did it openly. Because the credentials of real Christianity are public property.

God wants your life to be an open letter of testimony, not a secret code written in invisible ink that only fellow Christians can decipher. What a challenge to openness, to candour! It is the very essence of what the gospel is all about, says Paul. There can be nothing esoteric about it.

2. A man whose vocation demanded a public ministry (3:5ff)

> Not that we are competent in ourselves to claim anything for
> ourselves, but our competence [our qualification, if you like]
> comes from God. He has made us competent as ministers of
> a new covenant – not of the letter but of the Spirit; for the
> letter kills, but the Spirit gives life. Now if the ministry that
> brought death, which was engraved in letters on stone, came
> with glory, so that the Israelites could not look steadily at the
> face of Moses because of its glory, fading though it was, will
> not the ministry of the Spirit be even more glorious? (3:5-8).

Here Paul produces for his critics his strongest defence against their
ideas. He could see an argument flowing out of the discussion
between the old covenant and the new that would scotch the error of
their esoteric, secretive version of Christianity once and for all. It is
all tied up with the word 'glory'. Just observe how often it occurs in
verses 7-11.

We can define glory as 'a public manifestation of the presence
and character of God'. In the Old Testament it was closely associated with the fiery cloud that led the Jews in the wilderness and
covered Mount Sinai during the period of the law-giving. So brilliant was this cloud of glory that according to the book of Exodus,
when Moses came down from the mountain having been immersed
in it for forty days he shone himself. So intense was that radiance,
indeed, that the people were dazzled and he had to put a veil over his
face to hide the glory.

A young student once suggested to me that the Old Testament
record proved that what was actually happening on Mount Sinai
was some kind of nuclear reaction – Moses shone because he was
radioactive. If so, it would be good news for the Atomic Energy
Authority, because Moses went on to live for a hundred and twenty
years with no sign of leukaemia or radiation sickness! We must
leave that sort of silly speculation to films like *Raiders of the Lost
Ark*. The truth is that this was a supernatural incandescence, no more
describable in terms of nuclear physics than the incarnation of

Christ is describable in terms of genetic engineering. It was not
atomic radiation. It was divine glory. The fact that the Old Testament law was given amidst such a public manifestation was clear
evidence of its God-given character and immense significance.

But – says Paul – we Christians know that in spite of all that
splendour, the law of God was no real solution to the plight of men.
It did not save anybody. On the contrary, in an ironic way it
succeeded only in making them vulnerable to judgment. Verse 9: 'It
was a ministry that condemns men.' It was because of that, says
Paul, that the glory on Moses' face faded away in time. The Old
Testament was no permanent answer. It was just a stop-gap measure, a parenthesis in God's plan of salvation. It was not intended to
last for ever, it was pointing forward to something in the future,
something new.

To fully understand what Paul is getting at here, you need to read
the letters of Romans and Galatians. Paul seems to assume that his
readers were familiar with elements of his teaching that we find in
those other letters, so he does not elucidate further. Suffice it to say
here that in Paul's view the law was inadequate, because it could
only prescribe what men *ought* to do; it did not have the moral power
to enable them to do it. It was like a judge who jailed you for
bankruptcy, but had no advice at all on how you could get hold of the
money to pay your debts.

That is why he says in verse 6: 'The letter kills, but the Spirit
gives life.' That text has nothing whatsoever to do with the distinction that people sometimes draw between the 'letter of the law' and
'the spirit of the law', though it is often mistakenly quoted in that
kind of context. Nor is it an encouragement to allegorical techniques of biblical interpretation, though you will sometimes find it
used to support that idea too. What Paul means is that the law was
a purely *external* moral code; such a code, though it may be very
successful in exposing people's sin, is no use at all for cleansing
people's sin. What people need, if they are to be delivered from
condemnation of sin, is an *internal* moral renewal. The law must not
just be written in stone; the Spirit must write it on the heart.

And that, he says, is precisely what the New Covenant is all about. It is not a ministry that brings condemnation; it is a ministry that brings righteousness (verse 9). It is not just a temporary stop-gap, it is the ultimate solution. That is why Christianity is superior to Judaism. 'Why,' he says, 'I would much rather be called to be a minister of the church, than a minister of the synagogue any day. For the old covenant religion, for all its lofty revelation of God, is lethal; it kills, it condemns. Only the new covenant ministry of the Spirit has the power to give life, to make righteous.'

Now: since we Christians understand that, what about the glory? If the giving of the law, though it resulted in death, came amid such a splendid public manifestation of the presence of God that Moses' face shone – would you not expect the giving of the gospel, which has the power to bring life to humanity, to be associated with an even greater public manifestation? Indeed, you would, Paul says.

> If the ministry that condemns men is glorious, how much more glorious is the ministry that brings righteousness! ... And if what was fading away came with glory, how much greater is the glory of that which lasts! (3:9,11)

And that, says Paul, is precisely the reason I have no time for esoteric religion. 'Therefore, since we have such a hope, we are very bold, we are very outspoken, we use great freedom of speech.' Here is the rationale behind Paul's departure into this rather difficult theological backwater. I cannot help blazoning the gospel abroad, he says, any more than Moses could stop his face shining: it is of the nature of glory to irradiate the world, and the glory of the gospel is even more scintillating in this regard than the glory of the Ten Commandments.

To drive his point home, he develops his Old Testament exposition a little further.

> We are not like Moses, who would put a veil over his face to keep the Israelites from gazing at it while the radiance was fading away. But their minds were made dull, for to this day

> **the same veil remains when the old covenant is read.
> It has not been removed, because only in Christ is it
> taken away (3:13-14).**

'Do you know why Moses had to put a veil on his face?' asks
Paul. Whatever the human motivation might have been, the
Scripture records it because of its symbolic significance. That
veil was there because the glory of the old covenant was a
fading inadequate glory. The law, for all its value, did not
change hearts. Indeed, it only exacerbated the moral sclerosis
that affects the human race. Moses' veil was a symbol of the
spiritual veil that lies over the minds of fallen men and women
by nature. So impenetrable is that veil, Paul explains, that they
cannot understand the Bible properly. They cannot even understand the Ten Commandments that Moses gave. The power
of sin distorts and hides everything. Even now, he says, there
are thousands of people still blinded by a veil of incomprehen-
sion due to their hardness of heart.

But now all over the world, like London after the blackout,
the lights are going on, the curtains are being drawn back, light
is streaming into hearts and minds long shrouded in darkness;
because Christ has come.

> **Even to this day when Moses is read, a veil covers their
> hearts. But whenever anyone turns to the Lord, the
> veil is taken away (3:15-16).**

Paul is, I think, here alluding to Exodus 34:34, which says that
whenever Moses entered the Lord's presence he removed the
veil he wore when mixing with the people. Well, says Paul, do
you know who that Lord Jehovah is so far as we Christians are
concerned? He is the Spirit. The Lord to whom we turn is the
Spirit of Jesus, the Spirit of the new covenant written on hearts,
not stones.

> **Now the Lord is the Spirit, and where the Spirit of the
> Lord is, there is freedom (3:17).**

That is a slightly unexpected word: freedom. What sort of freedom does he mean? Is he referring to freedom from the condemnation of the law, about which he was speaking in verse 9? It's possible, but there is an alternative. The word 'freedom' could be a glance back to verse 12 and that word 'bold' which we considered earlier. In Greek, you recall, it means 'freedom of speech'. Perhaps the thrust of verse 17 then is something like this: 'This is the age of the Spirit. All need for veiling the word of God is passed. We have entered into an area of freedom. There may have been something legitimately esoteric about the religion of Moses; perhaps he needed to keep the glory secret, hidden behind the veil. Undisclosed mystery was an essential element of that old covenant dispensation which was looking forward to Christ. But no longer! The new covenant has come. The secret purpose of God have been revealed now, the mystery has been dispelled now, there can be no more drapes over the glory of God.'

One might respond, 'What glory of God? Moses' face shone; where is the phosphorescence of the new covenant?' I will tell you, says Paul:

> **We, who with unveiled faces all reflect the Lord's glory, are being transformed into his likeness with ever-increasing glory** (3:18).

The old covenant glory was a physical radiance adhering to the surface of Moses' face, because the old covenant blessing was law, and that could never get beneath the surface of human nature. But new covenant glory is a moral radiance that transforms the inner character of human beings, for the new covenant blessing is the Spirit, and he penetrates beneath the surface to the very heart of man. He reproduces not just a superficial shine on the face, but the very image of God embossed into human character, says Paul; and that is a glory which will never fade, and which will go on deepening as long as time shall last and into eternity.

That is why the church must never be regarded as merely a private club for people who share the same hobby. No! The church is a greenhouse for people who are all growing into the same likeness.

How can you possibly hide that? How can you possibly be secretive about a work of the Spirit as profound as that? Paul's vocation was to be a minister of the new covenant. And that means he had to be a publicist. Even if he said nothing, the glory would still be there. Where? In his life; in the life of his converts.

4

Why be a Preacher?
(2 Corinthians 4:1-15)

Therefore, since through God's mercy we have this ministry, we do not lose heart. Rather, we have renounced secret and shameful ways; we do not use deception, nor do we distort the word of God. On the contrary, by setting forth the truth plainly we commend ourselves to every man's conscience in the sight of God. And even if our gospel is veiled, it is veiled to those who are perishing. The god of this age has blinded the minds of unbelievers, so that they cannot see the light of the gospel of the glory of Christ, who is the image of God. For we do not preach ourselves, but Jesus Christ as Lord, and ourselves as your servants for Jesus' sake. For God, who said, "Let light shine out of darkness," made his light shine in our hearts to give us the light of the knowledge of the glory of God in the face of Christ.

But we have this treasure in jars of clay to show that this all-surpassing power is from God and not from us. We are hard pressed on every side, but not crushed; perplexed, but not in despair; persecuted, but not abandoned; struck down, but not destroyed. We always carry around in our body the death of Jesus, so that the life of Jesus may also be revealed in our body. For we who are alive are always being given over to death for Jesus' sake, so that his life may be revealed in our mortal body. So then, death is at work in us, but life is at work in you.

It is written: "I believed; therefore I have spoken." With that same spirit of faith we also believe and therefore speak, because we know that the one who raised the Lord Jesus from the dead will also raise us with Jesus and present us with you in his presence. All this is for your benefit, so that the grace that is reaching more and more people may cause thanksgiving to overflow to the glory of God (2 Corinthians 4:1-15).

'IT SEEMS A BIT OF A WASTE,' HE SAID.

I nodded. I could see his point. We were talking over coffee in the university laboratory where he and I had been working as colleagues for the best part of two years. Somehow our conversation had got round to what we were going to do next. He had shown me a letter he had just received, offering him a job in a scientific instrument company. The salary mentioned had so many zeroes on the end, I thought at first it was expressed in Italian lire rather than American dollars! Then he asked me about my plans.

'Well,' I said, 'I am thinking seriously about going into the Christian ministry.'

His eyes blinked. His coffee-cup froze in mid-air. For some moments he said nothing at all. Then he gulped slightly.

'It seems a bit of a waste,' he said.

I nodded. I could indeed see his point. For seven years I had been studying science, and in those pre-recession days well-qualified scientists were in demand. What is more, I enjoyed science, I was quite good at it. My parents had made considerable sacrifices to launch me on an academic career which they were certain would end nowhere short of a Nobel prize. To think of changing direction at this late stage! Well, it seemed lunacy! To throw away so much hard-won specialist knowledge. A bit of a waste? Well, frankly, that was an understatement.

What on earth was I doing even considering such a reckless move?

'Why be a preacher, Roy?' I asked myself.

During the years since that conversation, that question has sometimes come back to haunt me. And when it does I always read this passage once again, as I read it that same evening, after my colleague had gone home.

If anybody had reason to regret his decision to be a preacher, Paul did. He had a promising academic career in front of him too: lecturer in Old Testament at the university of Jerusalem. If he had gone on as he was going, he would have inherited Gamaliel's professorial chair for sure when the old boy died. Yet what did he do? He threw it all away in order to be a Christian missionary. His friends must have told him, 'It seems like a bit of a waste, Paul.' And what had his missionary work earned him? He tells us later in chapter 4 and again in chapter 6: worry, hardships, beatings, imprisonments, sleepless nights, poverty, sickness – and that is only half the list. It would not have been so bad if the churches he served had expressed some gratitude for all the sacrifice he had made, but half the time, they were a worse burden to him than anything else.

Take Corinth for instance, a city where he had endured relentless hostility and scorn from his fellow-countrymen the Jews for over eighteen months while he had stayed there and founded that first Christian congregation. It could only have been a few years at the most since he had left them, yet already trouble was brewing. Now, distracted by the anxiety of it all, he cannot concentrate on the evangelistic programme he has scheduled in Asia; he is uncharacteristically restless and disturbed (2:13).

'Why do I bother?' he must have been asking himself. 'Why on earth didn't I stay lecturing in Jerusalem? I could have been rich and famous by now. Whatever possessed me to embark on this crazy missionary adventure? It has ruined my career, it is ruining my health. If I die in my bed it will be a miracle, and all I get for it are treacherous stabs in the back from my own converts! What is the point of it all? Why be a preacher?'

In chapter 4 we find Paul answering that question. He is explaining his reason for being passionately committed to preaching, a commitment from which, he tells us, despite countless set-backs and disappointments he refuses to be deterred. Indeed, the key word of this passage is found at the beginning in verse 1 and the end in verse 16: 'We do not lose heart.' Bracketed between that repetition is an intensely personal piece of writing. You have only to scan it to note the predominance of first person pronouns. Paul is not engaging in abstract theological generalisation here. He is giving us his testimony as to why he was a preacher, and why he was determined to be nothing else. And when I read this passage as a young research student asking that same question, 'Why be a preacher?', I found that in some strange way Paul was speaking for me too. And my dearest wish is that among my readers may be those who, reading these words of Paul, will find them speaking for them also.

Why be a preacher? Because, Paul tells us, preaching is God's appointed method of bringing the light of Christ to men and women. Let us go through the passage together and see how he develops it.

> **Therefore, since through God's mercy we have this minis-try, we do not lose heart** (4:1).

It was always an amazement to Paul that God should have called him, of all people, to be a preacher; because, of course, in his unconverted days he had been a ruthless persecutor of the church. I imagine that is what he means when he says 'through the mercy of God we have received this ministry.' But it is remarkable how often the people who are most antagonistic before they are converted are those whom God calls to be champions in the pulpit later on. Perhaps it is only people who know from personal experience just how large the mercy of God is, that can with confidence invite other prodigals back into the Father's arms. Certainly, there is no doubt that these opening verses of Chapter 4 show the great sense of personal responsibility that Paul felt as a result of this vocation that God had placed upon him. Preaching, for him, was an immensely serious business.

> **We have renounced secret and shameful ways; we do not use deception, nor do we distort the word of God. On the contrary, by setting forth the truth plainly we commend ourselves to every man's conscience in the sight of God** (4:2).

You will remember that Paul is consciously defending his leader-ship style against certain rivals in this letter. And it seems that the same group of 'spiritual peddlers' (as he called them in 2:17) are on his mind as he writes this chapter. There were Christians around who, in Paul's estimation, did pursue 'secret and shameful ways'. There were preachers who, in Paul's judgment, did seek converts through 'deception' and by 'distorting the word of God'. Though the exact nature of this rival faction is the subject of interminable academic debate, I have argued that one of their characteristics was that they disapproved of the openness with which Paul preached in public.

They represented a more esoteric brand of Christianity. They liked to keep the Christian faith shrouded in a tantalising aura of mystery. Like all the other occult sects that proliferated in the Hellenistic world of that time, they saw themselves as salesmen marketing a new religious product. And they knew that in the social climate of the first century, the more mysterious and magical the advertising image they created then the more customers would be attracted and the more initiation fees they would be able to obtain. So they kept their Christianity hidden under seductive wraps.

They preached, of course. But it was most likely 'sales patter', the kind of empty rhetoric that was so fashionable and admired in that society. 'We can offer you secret *gnosis* that will lift you up to a higher level of consciousness; knowledge that will send you on a trip like no other trip you have ever experienced and will take you into the mysteries of God himself.'

Appealing, no doubt to first-century Greeks, but it was rather short on Christian doctrine. There was nothing about sin; nothing about judgment; nothing about the cross; not even, I suspect, very much about Jesus. No doubt if you had quizzed them they would have admitted they did believe in all these things; Paul does not call them heretics. So presumably they were, at least nominally, orthodox in their creed. It was their methodology Paul objected to. It was all too crafty, too devious, too shaped by the artful marketing techniques of the world, and for Paul that would not do. He had repudiated that kind of strategy of enticement the day he received his calling to be a preacher. The ministry God had called him to simply was not like that. We renounced, he says, all that disgraceful secrecy nonsense, all that subterfuge and adulteration of the gospel message. No, his method – if you could call it a method at all – was to tell people the straightforward, unvarnished facts.

We keep nothing up our sleeves, he says: 'We speak plainly.' We do not restrict ourselves to some inner circle of initiates, but 'commend ourselves to every man's conscience'. We do not twist our message to please our hearers, we speak 'the truth'. It is impossible for him to discharge the ministry God has given him on any other basis than one of total candour and unimpeachable integrity. And if someone challenges Paul by claiming that their techniques bring more public response than his preaching does, he has his answer ready:

> **Even if our gospel is veiled, it is veiled to those who are perishing. The god of this age has blinded the minds of unbelievers, so that they cannot see the light of the gospel of the glory of Christ, who is the image of God (4:3-4).**

The reference to 'veils' and 'glory' shows that Paul still has in mind that contrast he was drawing in chapter 3 between the old and new covenants. He claimed there that, extraordinary as it may seem, the Jewish people did not really understand their own Bible. There is a veil over their minds and hearts which spiritually blinds them: only when a person turns to Christ, does the Spirit of the Lord remove that veil (cf. 3:15-16).

Now in these verses he is generalising that point to include all non-Christians, not just the Jews. Anybody who hears the gospel message, he says, and does not make sense of it, is like a Jew reading the Old Testament law. He has spiritual cataracts over his eyes, and they prevent him from seeing what to Christian perception is so glaring and obvious – the glory of God in the face of Jesus.

Notice the agent of this spiritual cataract, if we may so call it. The 'god of this age' has blinded the minds of unbelievers. Many of the early Church Fathers interpreted that to mean 'the God who rules this age', namely the Lord God, God with a capital 'G'. And that is by no means impossible, because Paul in Romans 9 is not embarrassed to attribute unbelief directly to the decree of God when he speaks about Pharaoh's hardened heart: 'God has mercy on whom he wants to have mercy, and he hardens whom he wants to harden' (Rom. 9:18). But it has to be said that the phrase 'the god of this age' is a rather unlikely title for God himself. God is the king of all the ages, and it seems rather strange, almost inglorious – faint praise at best – to limit him to one.

Most modern commentators realise that and interpret the phrase differently. They say it means 'the god whom this age worships' – namely, the devil. He it is who blinds the minds of unbelievers. Again, that is far from an impossible view. Jesus himself in the parable of the Sower speaks of the devil's activity in stealing the word of the gospel from people's hearts before it has time to take root. And he himself calls the devil on one occasion 'the prince of this world'.

But I must say that I have never been fully convinced of that interpretation either. I know of nowhere else in the Bible where the word 'god' is attributed in that way to the devil. I would be surprised if that were Paul's intention. My own view is that this phrase is to be understood as what is technically called an 'appositional genitive'. That simply means that 'god of this age' means 'the god who consists of this age'. In other words, people make this age their god. And that is what renders them blind.

There is another example of such an appositional genitive in verse 6: 'the light of the knowledge of the glory of God' – light which consists of the knowledge of the glory of God. It is quite a regular way of interpreting a genitive in Greek. And if you take it that way then Paul is saying that it is an idolatrous preoccupation with the material things of this passing world, which renders the spiritual things of the next world undetectable to men's gaze. Later on in verse 18, Paul speaks about the way he fixes his eyes not on the things that are seen, but on the things that are unseen. The unbeliever's problem is they do the opposite. They fix their eyes on the things that are seen, the temporal things, and that renders them insensitive to those eternal things that are invisible except to the eye of faith.

That interpretation seems to me to be more consistent with the Bible's assertion that though unbelieving men and women are victims of ignorance, it is a wilful ignorance. Though they are spiritually blind, it is a culpable blindness. It is because they have chosen to worship that which is less than God that God has given them over to a darkened mind, and the devil finds it so easy to steal the word of God from their hearts. So while it is perfectly possible to see God's decree and the devil's malice behind their unbelief, we are not to be narrowly deterministic about it. People are numbered among the perishing because they turn their backs on the obvious, not because they are trapped by an inexorable fate, whether of divine or demonic origin.

Still, however you read the phrase, the central thrust of verses 3 and 4 is essentially the same. Paul is pointing out that it is not because of any deficiency in his preaching that people remain unbelievers. It is because of a spiritual barrier in their own souls. The gospel is not a mystery to them because he kept it a mystery, but because they cannot and will not understand it; as John puts it in his Gospel, the Light is there blazing away for all to see. The problem is that sinful men and women prefer to live in the darkness.

If that is the case, one might respond, how does anybody ever become a Christian? Surely we are all in the same boat as far as this is concerned – including Paul – for surely we are all spiritually blind by nature. 'Absolutely right,' replies Paul, 'I could not agree more. The only reason my preaching has any saving effect at all in men and women is because God chooses to accompany it with something I cannot provide: his own miracle of spiritual illumination.'

> **We do not preach ourselves, but Jesus Christ as Lord, and ourselves as your servants for Jesus' sake. For God, who said, 'Let light shine out of darkness,' made his light shine in our hearts to give us the light of the knowledge of the glory of God in the face of Christ (4:5-6).**

That is why the believer sees it: because God has made his light shine in their heart. Paul of course is still talking here in the first person, so verse 6 may well be a direct reference to his own conversion experience, when he saw the light on the Damascus road in a very literal sense. 'Who are you, Lord?' he asked of that blazing vision that dazzled him. 'I am Jesus,' came the reply. And it is surely significant that he left that encounter physically blind, but spiritually enlightened for the first time in his life.

For Paul such words were more than mere metaphor; they were a personal testimony to what had happened to him. That experience, he tells us here, shaped the whole tenor of his subsequent preaching ministry. 'We do not preach ourselves, but Jesus Christ as Lord, and ourselves as servants for Jesus' sake.' It is not Paul's gifts, rhetoric, charm, personality, advertising skills or evangelistic techniques that bring men and women to conversion. 'It is face-to-face encounter with Jesus, the same Jesus who met me. So I just preach him. I tell people who he is and what he has done, and again and again, as I do that, God by his Spirit takes the veil away from their hearts, and they see what that day on the Damascus road I saw, the glory of God shining in the face of Jesus. Why,' he says, 'it feels just like pulling the bedroom curtains in the morning: gloom gives way to dawn!'

The vast majority of commentators take verse 6 as a reference to the opening words of Genesis. If that is correct then it is a powerful analogy that Paul is drawing here. He is saying that conversion involves an act of divine initiative as awesomely sovereign as the act of creation itself. God says to our hearts, 'Let there be light,' and there is light; and from that moment a new world begins.

However, it is worth noting that there is another possibility. In the original language, verse 6 bears more similarity to Isaiah 9:2 than it does to Genesis 1:3. 'The people walking in darkness have seen a great light; on those living in the land of darkness a light has dawned' – that very word. If Paul has Isaiah in mind rather than Genesis, then it is not so much an analogy to the Old Testament account of creation we have here as an example of the fulfilment of Messianic prophecy.

But however you take it, the implication, it seems to me, is just as thrilling, though unfortunately our translation rather mars it. What Paul actually says is not 'God *makes* the light that illumines a Christian heart' but 'God *is* the light'. It is God *himself* who has shone in our hearts. What we gain in the face of Jesus is not just the gift of spiritual insight; it is the vision of deity. Mystics down through the ages have always talked about it. 'Here it is!' says Paul.

Those cheap peddlers of the gospel! They may talk about the secret gnosis that they can offer people, but Paul has some 'knowledge' too: the light of the knowledge of the glory of God. He quite deliberately takes up gnostic vocabulary there and throws it back in their faces. 'I offer this knowledge not wrapped in mystical hocus-pocus; I offer it straight, in language nobody can misunderstand. I offer it in the face of Jesus to any and all to whom God gives eyes to see him.'

You say, Why be a preacher? Well, there is no calling on earth more noble. This is surely why Spurgeon said his pulpit was more desirable to him than the throne of England. Preaching is the event in which thousands upon thousands find their Damascus road. Paul's preaching was a real eye-opener, in more senses than one. It is God's method of bringing the light of Christ to men and women.

Perhaps you begin to see why this passage meant so much to me when I was considering embarking on a preaching ministry. In fact it is hard for me to express in a few words all these few verses have meant to me down through the years as I have thought about them. We are told by any number of people today that preaching is doomed. It is simply not worth the effort, they say. Again and again, when people have told me things like that, I have found this passage has encouraged me. 'We do not lose heart,' says Paul.

No, we do not!

1. Paul's words restore my confidence in the characteristics of good preaching

One reason preaching gets a bad press these days is because there is an incredible amount of bad preaching around. Some of it is bad simply because it is boring; it is an extraordinary thing to be able to make the glorious gospel of Christ sound monotonous, and yet there are a good many preachers who seem to be able to achieve that with remarkable regularity! I am reminded of the comment made about the notorious Reverend Frederick Morris, the nineteenth-century preacher, 'Listening to him is like to trying to eat pea soup with a fork'! The result of preaching like that, of course, is that people come to church expecting to be bored. The sermon becomes the Protestant equivalent of flagellation, a painful penance to be endured for the sake of church-going respectability. The number of people who mentally switch off as soon as the sermon begins, in anticipation of boredom to come, is lamentable. And those who grow up in Christian families, where they are subjected to bad preaching from a young age, are among the worst affected.

But boring preaching, although it is a terrible crime, is not the worst crime perpetrated in the pulpit. There are far worse forms of bad preaching. There is what Paul mentions here, for instance: deception and the distortion of God's word. It is all too easy for a preacher, in a laudable desire to get a response from hard hearts, to compromise his message in some way, to water it down and adapt it to make it more acceptable to his hearers.

He can leave out all the nasty parts – hell and all that stuff! He can leave out the demanding parts about repentance. He can leave out the difficult parts about the incarnation and atonement and so forth. He can replace them with lots of appealing carrots, by which to bribe his audience – promises of healing to the sick, promises of jobs to the unemployed, promises of rice to the hungry. He can talk about political issues. In a university town he can pad his sermon out with quotes from the philosophers. He can talk about existentialism, psychoanalysis, Adam Smith and Karl Marx, and flatter the ears of his hearers with how awfully avant-garde they are to be able to listen to all this stuff.

Or if none of that will do, he can always appropriate the technique of the anecdotal preacher and lead from his announced text into a whole patter of stories – some amusing, some touching, but all entertaining and all connected in some tenuous way with a blessed thought or two that might have some link, remotely, with the text from which he began. Such preaching may not be boring in the least. It may be conducted with great oratory and skill, and lead people into thinking they are actually hearing a Christian sermon when in fact they are hearing nothing of the kind. They are being deceived; the word of God is being distorted. Such a preacher is just a peddler, a salesman looking for a popular line to hawk.

Good preaching

What are the characteristics of good preaching? We find them delineated here in this passage.

First, *integrity*. 'We do not use deception.' There can be no disguising of the truth.

Second, *fidelity*. 'We do not distort the word of God.' We tell it to people as it is, every bit of it, without jumping over the awkward verses.

Third, *intelligibility*. 'By setting forth the truth plainly' – no woolliness in our presentation. We talk the language of the people so that they can understand it.

Fourthly, and by no means, last, *humility*: 'We do not preach ourselves, but Jesus Christ as Lord, and ourselves as your servants for Jesus' sake' (4:5). Of all forms of bad preaching, the worst is the kind of preaching that glorifies the preacher, and I fear that it is far from rare. Of course, up to a point preachers cannot avoid the fanclub syndrome – Paul had fans, as did Peter and Apollos. But some preachers actually encourage such adulation, and design their ministry so as to foster it. Sometimes they do it by making sure a very large portrait photograph of themselves appears as often as possible in the publicity. Some do it by filling their sermons with stories about how God has used them in this and that person's life. And some do it, sadly, by running down other preachers from the pulpit, cultivating very subtly but very definitely the impression that theirs is the only church in the area, if not in the entire country where the authentic gospel can be heard. And the result is always the same: the Christian personality cult.

These preachers are not preaching Christ at all but projecting themselves. No, says Paul, that is not my style. I do not expect to be treated like a celebrity everywhere I go. If I must talk about myself at all, it is as your slave (that is the word he uses) for Jesus' sake. And it was because of that fundamental humility in Paul that the perfidy of this Corinthian church, though it upset him, did not demoralise him. It did not make him lose heart. Paul's ego was not at stake in his preaching. He was secure enough in his divine vocation to be humble as well as candid. Good preaching always is.

2. Paul's words restore my confidence in the effectiveness of preaching

Another of the reasons that preaching is given little credibility today is much subtler and better-informed than simply the complaint that preachers are boring. Some say that even if the preaching is good, it is still not worth doing, because it does not do any good. This kind of comment comes from researchers in the field of communication. They have proved by their research that monodirectional communication (which is what preaching is) can reinforce attitudes and beliefs already held but can only very rarely effect real change in people's opinions. This is a facet, they say of human psychology. Monologue does not change anybody; so if you want to convert people, you have to stop preaching and use small group techniques or one-to-one dialogue instead..

Of course, if this proposition is accepted, the conclusion that you are forced to draw is that Jesus and the apostles showed a singular lack of awareness of basic human psychology when they chose the word 'preaching' (proclamation) to convey their understanding of evangelism. A preacher – *kerux* in the Greek – is a herald, and a herald is precisely a one-way communicator; he does not dialogue, he announces a message he has received. But if our communication experts are correct, announcements do not change anybody. Where is the flaw in their reasoning? I do not believe that the flaw lies in the research, which I am sure is quite correct. It lies in the theology. For people who argue like this are assuming that Christian preaching is analogous to a marketing exercise. You have your product: the gospel. You have your consumers: the congregation. And the preacher is the salesman. It is his job to overcome consumer resistance and persuade people to buy.

According to Paul, there is one very simple but overwhelming reason why that analogy is not a good one. The preacher does not overcome consumer resistance. He cannot. Consumer resistance is far too large for any preacher to overcome. All the preacher does, Paul says, is to expose that resistance in its formidable impenetrability. If our gospel is veiled, it is veiled to those who are perishing. The god of this age has blinded their minds and 'they cannot see the light of the gospel of the glory of Christ'.

It is such an important point. Jesus made it too in the parable of the Sower. A man went out and sowed the seed, said Jesus. Some fell on the path, some fell on the stones, some fell among the weeds, and some fell on good ground. Notice the way he structures his story: one sower, four soils. The sowing of the seed reveals differences of receptivity in the soil. But if our communication expert were to tell the parable, it would be the other way round. There would be one homogeneous soil, and four different sowers. Sower One would have a particular evangelistic technique, but it would be no good. Then Sower Two would use his method, but that would not work either. Sower Three would next use his particular evangelistic style, but unfortunately it would have very little effect, and then finally, there would be Sower Four who had his communication technique right, and he alone would obtain a harvest.

But that is not how it is. Christian conversion is not the result of human persuasion. According to Paul, it is a manifestation of divine grace. 'God who said, "Let light shine out of darkness," made his light shine in our hearts to *give* us the light of the knowledge of God in the face of Christ.'

That, of course, is why monologue is actually the ideal communication technique. For the function of the word is to make the person, in whom God has already been secretly at work by his Spirit, self-conscious of their salvation. The preacher does not save anybody. He is an instrument whereby people who are being saved become aware of the fact. Evangelism has to be proclamation because preaching is a sacrament of the divine sovereignty. God kindles spiritual life in souls by his Spirit, and then rejoices in their free, uncoerced, spontaneous response to his word when they hear it preached.

To be honest, the trouble with much evangelism today is that it is built on the fallacious – even heretical – assumption, that anybody can and will respond to the gospel if only it is presented to them in an appropriate fashion. It is not true. It is not what Paul says in verse 3 about spiritual blindness. In the preaching event it is the quality of the soil, not the quality of the preacher that is primarily being displayed. The word of the cross is folly to those who are perishing, said Paul; that was his experience, great preacher though he was. But to those who are being saved, it is the power of God. The preached word discriminates between the perishing and the saved in that way.

Do not misunderstand me. Of course the preacher uses argument, logic and appeal, because God speaks to us as rational beings. But the hard fact is that no amount of argument, or logic, or appeal will ever change a person's receptivity to God's word. If we find somebody receiving God's word and understanding it, it is not a triumph of the preacher's power of communication. It is a triumph of the Spirit, who has secretly transformed that person's heart. God has made his light shine there; he has illumined them. Preaching reveals that transformation but it cannot produce it.

Of course we do not like this. For a start, it robs us of our best excuse for our rejection of the gospel: that 'the preacher was no good'. What is more, it deflates the preacher's pride, because it means that really he is nothing very special. It is God who gives the increase; it is God who prepares the soil; it is God who opens the eyes. But this is how it is, says Paul. Preaching will be effective, not because as an instrument of human persuasion it is the best means – it is not, as modern psychology knows –but because it is God's chosen method whereby he opens people's eyes and brings them to an awareness that they are his saved people.

That is why it is such a solemn thing to hear God's word. Every time we come and hear it we are judging ourselves. That word is discriminating between us, saved or perishing. If we find the barest inkling of understanding of spiritual things being given to us as we read this letter of Paul's, if we find the barest hint of a desire to obey what we find there – well praise God for it. Fan that little glimmer of spiritual sensitivity in your hearts into a flame, because there is no blessing in this universe more precious than light. And God is the only one who can give it.

3. Paul's words restore my confidence in the necessity for preaching
There is a third reason people disparage preaching today, and it goes like this: 'People won't listen to preaching these days.'

If I have been told that once, I have been told it a thousand times. 'It demands too much concentration in the television age. If you want to attract non-Christians to the church, you must do away with long sermons. Bring in drama; bring in music groups; bring in films. Create an atmosphere of celebration. What you have got to do is to think about the way you package the gospel. Look at the world of entertainment; see what people find enjoyable. Look at the world of advertising; see what people find persuasive. Then mould your presentation of Christianity in the same way!'

I must be frank. I am very far from being opposed to drama, or music, or celebration, or films, or anything else of that nature. They all have something to contribute to the church's evangelistic task, and I do not deny it. But I will not have them regarded as a substitute for preaching. And I say that not because I am a preacher worried that I might lose my job! I say it because I believe it is the clear implication of what Paul is saying in these verses. 'By setting forth the truth plainly we commend ourselves to every man's conscience in the sight of God.'

That is, Paul says, how the gospel ought to be made known to people. There is such a thing as 'the truth'. The job of the evangelist is to press that truth on people's minds and on people's consciences in the plainest possible way. So the test of evangelistic methodology is not, 'How much did the non-Christians enjoy all that?' That is irrelevant. The test is, 'How much did they learn from it?' Not 'How electric was the atmosphere?', but 'How clear was the gospel?'

I am not saying that we must be indifferent to the quality of our evangelistic presentation. I have a great deal of sympathy with people who feel they cannot invite their non-Christian friends to this or that church because of its cliché-ridden language and old-fashioned hymns. But it is simply not true to say that people will not listen to preaching. If people are being awakened spiritually to their need of God, they will listen. If they are not being awakened to such a spiritual concern, no amount of gospel entertainment or evangelistic gimmickry will make them listen. We are not in the job of persuading people; we are in the job of watching God open blind eyes.

Do you see the difference? Drama, music, film and celebration may all complement preaching and add credibility to the Christian message. They may illustrate the joy of the Christian message and highlight its relevance. I am for all those things. But they cannot possibly communicate the Christian message as plainly and unambiguously as you can by preaching. And that is really what people need to have. 'Setting forth the truth plainly we commend ourselves to every man's conscience.' That is why Jesus preached; that is why Paul preached; that is why every revival the church has ever known has been led by preachers.

Maybe there are some among my readers who feel that God may be calling them to be preachers. I do not want you to jump to hasty conclusions based on the romantic ideas many people have about preaching. It is no bed of roses. Read the rest of this letter and you will know that. But I do not want you to soft-pedal that call, either. Do not let the bad preaching you have heard demoralise you. Do not let the negative comments you hear about preaching discourage you. Do not let the church's present neglect of preaching dissuade you. If in the mercy of God you are receiving a call to preach, do not lose heart.

Yes, it may involve quite a lot of sacrifice. But at the end of the day, you will not feel it to be a waste.

5

What Happens After Death?
(2 Corinthians 4:16-5:8)

Therefore we do not lose heart. Though outwardly we are wasting away, yet inwardly we are being renewed day by day. For our light and momentary troubles are achieving for us an eternal glory that far outweighs them all. So we fix our eyes not on what is seen, but on what is unseen. For what is seen is temporary, but what is unseen is eternal.

Now we know that if the earthly tent we live in is destroyed, we have a building from God, an eternal house in heaven, not built by human hands. Meanwhile we groan, longing to be clothed with our heavenly dwelling, because when we are clothed, we will not be found naked. For while we are in this tent, we groan and are burdened, because we do not wish to be unclothed but to be clothed with our heavenly dwelling, so that what is mortal may be swallowed up by life. Now it is God who has made us for this very purpose and has given us the Spirit as a deposit, guaranteeing what is to come.

Therefore we are always confident and know that as long as we are at home in the body we are away from the Lord. We live by faith, not by sight. We are confident, I say, and would prefer to be away from the body and at home with the Lord (2 Corinthians 4:16-5:8).

I huddle warmly inside my corner bed
Watching the other patients sipping tea
I wonder why I am so long getting well
And why it is that no one will talk to me.

The nurses are so kind, they brush my hair
On the days I feel too ill to read or sew
I smile and chat, try not to show my fear
But they will not tell me what I want to know

The visitors come, I see their eyes
Become embarrassed as they pass my bed
What lovely flowers, they say, then hurry on
In case their faces show what can't be said

The surgeon comes with student retinue
Mutters to sister, deaf to my mute plea
I want to tell them of this dread I feel inside
But they are all too kind to talk to me

The chaplain passes on his weekly round
A friendly smile and calm untroubled brow
He speaks with deep sincerity of life
I'd like to speak of death, but don't know how.

That poem, entitled somewhat cynically 'Terminal Care', appeared some years ago in *The Nursing Mirror*. It is a most moving expression of the inadequacy of our twentieth century, in spite of all the advances we have made in medical technology, to cope with the cold statistical fact that one hundred percent of all human beings sooner or later die. Why is that thought so unacceptable to us? Why do we all find it so difficult to even utter the word 'death'? Why is it we cloak the whole subject in this monstrous conspiracy of silence? One modern writer has described this as 'the universal human repression of our day'. He says it is the reality we dare not face, to escape which we create vast barricades of psychological defence. Death for the modern man, he says, is 'muffled up in illusions.'

Part of the answer must be, I think, that we treat death in this way because we are not sure what happens when we die. Death, as Hamlet remarked, is:

> The undiscover'd country from whose bourn
> No traveller returns, puzzles the will,
> And makes us rather bear those ills we have
> Than fly to others that we know not of. (Hamlet, Act 3 scene 1)

If only we knew with assurance what lies on the other side of the grave, we would dare to speak of death with less embarrassment. But though there are very few modern men and women who are afraid of hell, there are many who are afraid of death. These days it is not so much conscience as ignorance that (to quote Hamlet again) 'doth make cowards of us all'.

In this chapter I would like to dispel some of that ignorance, and perhaps the cowardice that goes with it. For we come to a passage in which Paul wants to tell us what happens when a Christian dies.

For him it was no longer a subject for speculation. Something tremendous had happened that had taken life after death out of the realm of conjecture or superstition, and moved it into the realm of established fact. Jesus Christ had been raised from the dead. For Paul this was no pious myth. It was an historical event attested by hundreds of eye-witnesses, including Paul himself.

Paul understood that this resurrection was no isolated occurrence or strange anomaly. It was the precursor of an even more momentous event: the general resurrection of all the people of God.

> **We know that the one who raised the Lord Jesus from the dead will also raise us with Jesus and present us with you in his presence (4:14).**

That confidence transformed the prospect of death for Paul. For him it could not be a repression wrapped in a conspiracy of silence; death was a conquered enemy now, so trivial, so innocuous, that he could mock it like a man brushing a troublesome mosquito from his brow.

> Where, O death, is your victory?
> Where, O death, is your sting?
> ... Thanks be to God! He gives us the victory through our Lord Jesus Christ (1 Cor. 15:55,57)

Our study will not be in vain if at the end of it we are able to talk about death with something approaching Paul's unembarrassed candour; for there are few people who can do so today.

The passage we are studying in this chapter has two parts, divided by the chapter break. In 4:7-18, Paul is telling us about life beyond death as a *present experience*. In 5:1-8 he is telling us about life beyond death as a *future hope*.

1. Life beyond death as a present experience

> We always carry around in our body the death of Jesus, so that the life of Jesus may also be revealed in our body. For we who are alive are always being given over to death for Jesus' sake, so that his life may be revealed in our mortal body (4:10-11).

It may seem strange to speak of life beyond death as a present experience: surely, by definition, you have to die first to get it. But the fascinating thing is that according to Paul that is not so. For him the life of the world to come is already at work in the Christian here and now. Indeed, its vitality is something of which Paul was immensely conscious, because of the rigours and dangers of his apostolic ministry.

'Great though the gospel I have been given to preach is,' Paul is saying, 'I am painfully aware of the limitations placed upon my ministry by the frailty of my human nature.' In verse 7 he uses the rather touching image of 'jars of clay'. He may have in mind the kind of earthenware lamps that were common in those days. Or, it has been suggested, he may be casting his eyes back to that triumphal procession he spoke of in Chapter 2, because captured booty was often paraded in such a victory celebration, carried in Grecian urns. But whatever the picture Paul had in mind, he is confessing in a typically self-effacing manner that the glorious light of the knowledge of God, of which he has spoken in verse 6, is enshrined in a most inglorious and unworthy human receptacle. 'I am,' says Paul, 'the insignificant tissue paper in which the precious jewel of the gospel is wrapped. I am the fragile eggshell in which the living seed of the gospel is incubated. I am the worn and frayed cable by which the mighty energy of the gospel is transmitted: a jar of clay.' But Paul says it is better that way; because in a strange way, his weakness has the effect of enhancing his effectiveness as an evangelist rather than decreasing it.

If the gospel succeeds it is not because of the dynamism of the preacher. It can only be because of some intrinsically supernatural dimension in the message. We have this treasure in jars of clay to show that this all-surpassing power comes from God, not us. And in the series of epigrams that follow (verse 8 ff.), Paul gives some examples of that power at work. 'I am hard-pressed on every side,' he says, 'squeezed into all kinds of tight corners, pressurised by countless stresses outside my control: but I have never felt strait-jacketed yet. I am hard-pressed, yes − but not crushed.'

'I often become perplexed in my ministry,' he says − and the verb suggests that all ideas have fled, that the mind has been left vacant and bewildered, utterly at a loss. 'But,' says Paul, 'though at times I have been at my wits' end in that way, I have never been reduced to total hopelessness. Perplexed, yes, but not in despair. I have been persecuted, and hunted like a wild animal. On occasions I have even been struck down, literally, thrown prostrate as by a heavy blow. But I have never given up, because I have never felt abandoned. I have always managed to beat the count and get on my feet again, no matter how hard the punch. They can beat me up, but they cannot eliminate me. "They can knock me down, but they cannot knock me out" (J. B. Phillips translation).'

I feel, says Paul, rather like that saint of old who wrote Psalm 116: he had experienced mortal danger, too. But in spite of all the human opposition, all the physical threats he faced against his life, there was something within him that could not stop trusting God and testifying in public to that trust. Paul quotes him in verse 13: 'I believed; therefore I have spoken.'

With that same spirit of faith we also believe. And therefore we go on preaching.

And if you ask me to explain how frail old Paul managed to demonstrate that extraordinary physical and emotional resilience to all the hardships and afflictions that came his way, I will tell you: it is the power of the resurrection.

We always carry around in our body the death of Jesus, so that the life of Jesus may also be revealed in our body. For we who are alive are always being given over to death for Jesus' sake, so that his life may be revealed in our mortal body (4:10-11).

Do you see? For Paul, the resurrection was not confined to some future life beyond the grave. It was already part of his experience. There was a kind of symbiosis between him and Jesus; they died and lived together. Like spiritual Siamese twins, they were fused by a union that linked them in their experience and in their destiny.

'And,' says Paul, 'the very persistence and vigour of my Christian stand as an apostle, in spite of the all-too-obvious feebleness of this clay pot which is me, is proof of the spiritual reality of this living Christ within me, to which I testify. Death is at work in us – yes, but life is at work in you. It is all for your benefit. So that the grace that is reaching more and more people may cause thanksgiving to overflow to the glory of God' (verse 15).

'That is what is so remarkable,' he says: 'the more battered I am, the more successful my ministry seems to be and the more glory goes to God for the multiplying numbers of people who receive the grace of God through me.'

We must not misunderstand what Paul is saying in these verses. He is not engaging in the kind of naive triumphalism that says, 'If you are a real Christian and trust God hard enough, your problems will all be over.' Nor is he saying that the resurrection power of Jesus guaranteed healing for him when he was sick, release for him when he was in prison, or rescue for him when he was under threat of execution. Quite the contrary: Paul is all too aware of his physical and emotional vulnerability: he is an ordinary human being, a clay pot, with a mortal body – 'a body that dies' (verse 11). He is not some heroic Achilles, rendered impregnable by magic. You only had to look at Paul to see the scars and the wear and tear, the sheer exhaustion which his missionary ordeals had inflicted on him. 'We always carry around in our body the death of Jesus,' he says. There is not much exaggeration in that. There were times, I suspect, when Paul did look only a little fitter than a man who was in the process of being crucified.

So we are not to think of Paul as one of those glib, pseudo-Christian salesmen we have encountered in previous chapters with their cheap and shoddy gospel of health-and-wealth for all. There can be no immunity for the Christian from troubles, any more than there could be immunity for Jesus from the cross. The difference Christianity makes is not in our outward circumstances. Those may be made all the more harrowing and difficult because we are Christians, just as they were for Paul. The difference Christianity makes is to our *inward* resources.

> **Therefore we do not lose heart. Though outwardly we are wasting away, yet inwardly we are being renewed day by day. For our light and momentary troubles are achieving for us an eternal glory that far outweighs them all** (4:16-17).

To understand those verses properly you have to realise that according to the New Testament, a Christian is a person who lives in two dimensions at once. On one level, outwardly, he lives in this world and is therefore vulnerable to pain and trouble like anybody else.

But on another level, he inwardly participates in the world to come, the world of heaven, the world of glory. This inner life is the miracle of which Jesus spoke to Nicodemus when he said, 'You must be born again. Not outwardly and physically by going back into your mother's womb, but inwardly and spiritually by the Spirit of God' (cf. John 3).

That is why we can say that life beyond death is not merely something in the future for the Christian, it is part of present experience. Here and now, inwardly, the Christian participates in the power of the resurrection. 'It is that inner experience,' says Paul, 'that gives me the resources by which I demonstrate such a resilience to outward trouble. That is the secret of my toughness.' After all, he says, what are these slings and arrows of outrageous fortune that afflict him? Seen in the light of the resurrection they are trivial, ephemeral flea-bites. In comparison with the tons of glory that await him, they are like insignificant dust on the weighing-scales. In comparison with the vast millennia of eternity that await him, they are like the fleeting shadows cast by passing clouds on a sunny day.

Of course the trouble with unbelievers, as we saw back in verse 4, is that their idolatrous preoccupation with this world has blinded them to the reality of the next one. They cannot see it, because their eyes are fixed on material, obvious things. But not us Christians; we have been inwardly illuminated by the light of Christ.

So we fix our eyes not on what is seen, but on what is unseen. For what is seen is temporary, but what is unseen is eternal (4:18).

Tell me, how do you feel about growing old?

There has probably not been a culture in the entire history of the world more paranoid about the ageing process than ours. A comedian once said that the most frightening thing about middle age is the knowledge that you will outgrow it. Everybody wants to live a long time, but nobody wants to be old. It is not difficult to understand why. Old age brings infirmity. Your eyes grow dim, your ears deaf, your limbs stiff; your memory lets you down, the old grey cells

do not work as quickly as they used to – even your bladder becomes
an embarrassment to you! Old age brings disfigurement too. The
once-handsome physique grows shapeless and bent; the once-
beautiful complexion acquires wrinkles. That lovely head of hair
grows grey or falls out altogether, and the cosmetic remedies for this
inexorable process of uglification become more and more expensive and less and less effective.

Perhaps worst of all, old age brings a kind of morbid foreboding.
Maurice Chevalier said that old age is not so bad when you consider
the alternative. Nobody likes to face up to that! Yet the process of
ageing stamps on every creaking joint the awareness of the depressing advance of death. It is not surprising that people are so neurotic
about staying young.

So, how do you feel about getting old? We know how the apostle
Paul felt. He tells us himself.

**We do not lose heart. Though outwardly we are wasting
away, yet inwardly we are being renewed day by day** (4:16).

There was no geriatric self-pity in Paul. Physical infirmity was a
nuisance, admittedly, but it was no cause for despair. Why? Because
old age – quite literally – is not the end of the world. Not of the
Christian's world, at any rate. The Christian has his mind fixed upon
another world.

'Inwardly we are being renewed day by day.' I don't care how
old you are or how weak you feel; if you are a Christian then the
resurrection life of Jesus is glowing inside you like an atomic pile,
radiating the energy of the world to come. I do not promise you that
it will take away your rheumatism. I cannot promise you it will do
anything about that bald spot which is beginning to get so conspicu-
ous. I cannot pretend that source of new world energy is going to
prevent the day coming for you as for everybody else, when your
fragile heart finally abandons the struggle to beat. If we are honest,
we will have to admit that the greatest and most godly of Christian
men and women sometimes end their lives in conditions of physical

and intellectual dilapidation. And it may happen to us, no matter how many beauty treatments we may have or how many gymnasia we subscribe to.

But I want to tell you this. If you are a Christian, such things are really not worth worrying about. In fact, to fret about getting old is to live like a pagan, blinded by the visible things of this world, when you should be living like a Christian, a believer in the resurrection of Jesus Christ, fixing your gaze on the invisible things of the next world. Problems of old age pale into insignificance before verses 17 and 18. Outwardly you may be getting nearer and nearer to death, but inwardly, you are getting nearer and nearer to glory. So be like Paul; do not lose heart. 'Grow old along with me,' says Browning. 'The best is yet to be.'

2. Life beyond the grave as future hope

> Now we know that if the earthly tent we live in is destroyed, we have a building from God, an eternal house in heaven, not built by human hands (5:1).

'Let's imagine the worst,' says Paul. 'Let's imagine I die. Let's imagine that this biochemical fabric to which I have been so attached for the past fifty years or so is finally dissolved into its constituent atoms. Let's suppose that this tent of my body which I live in is compulsorily dismantled, and death like an unsympathetic landlord tells me I have got to find new accommodation. Would such an eviction order make me homeless? Not at all,' says Paul. 'For I have a far superior dwelling at my disposal, and unlike my present property it is permanent. An eternal house, not a temporary tent. What is more, it is located in a much classier neighbourhood! In heaven, not on earth. Quite frankly,' says Paul, 'I cannot wait to move in. Meanwhile, we groan, longing to be clothed with our heavenly dwelling ...'

That much at any rate is plain from these first verses of chapter 5. Paul has moved on from talking about life after death as a present experience to talking about it as a future hope. And though his metaphors are strangely mixed – we normally put on clothes, not buildings – it is not difficult to grasp his point: that Christians do not need to fear death, because for a Christian, death is no more traumatic than moving house or buying a new suit. It is merely a change, and a change for the better at that.

Yet it has to be said that when one looks at the detail of these verses, a number of interpretative problems arise.

(a) The building from heaven (5:1-2)

For example, what precisely is the 'building from heaven'?

At the risk of oversimplifying a good deal of academic discussion, I think we can be reasonably sure that this metaphor refers to the spiritual body that Paul believed every Christian would receive when he or she was raised from the dead, and which he discusses at considerable length in Chapter 15 of his first letter to the Corinthians. Contrary to popular myth, Christians are not going to spend eternity plucking harps on celestial clouds, dressed in some kind of ethereal negligee. Paul insists in that passage that they will have new bodies, suited for the new world that God has prepared for them to inhabit. Furthermore, as he is at pains to stress in our passage here, there will be nothing insubstantial about those new bodies; if anything, they will be more concrete than our present ones: permanent buildings rather than temporary tents.

You may wonder where Paul got such an extraordinary idea as 'a spiritual body'. The answer can only be that he got it from the same place he got all his information about life beyond the grave: from the resurrection of Jesus. When Jesus was raised from the dead, he had a body – changed in its physical properties, true, but a body nevertheless. What is more, he took that resurrection body to heaven with him. And Paul expected that one day the frailty and weakness of his own body would be exchanged for a new glorified spiritual body, just like that of the risen Jesus. He makes that quite clear in Philippians 3:20-21: 'We eagerly await a Saviour from [heaven], the Lord Jesus Christ, who ... will transform our lowly bodies so that they will be like his glorious body.' That is a very good commentary on 2 Corinthians 5:1.

But this identification of the 'heavenly house' with the 'spiritual body' raises a second question.

(b) The receiving of the 'heavenly house' (5:2-4)
When did Paul expect to receive this spiritual body, this 'heavenly house'?

In both 1 Corinthians 15 and Philippians 3:20, Paul speaks of the spiritual body as if Christians are going to receive it at the end of the world when Jesus returns. But these verses in 2 Corinthians 5 do not refer to the second coming of Jesus, but to the hypothetical possibility of Paul dying before then. So how does Paul's hope of a resurrection body relate to what happens when a Christian dies? To put it frankly: does he get his spiritual body straightaway, or does he have to wait around for it until the end of the world?

This is a vexed question that has puzzled many Christians. The only specific teaching we have on it is 2 Corinthians 5:2-4. Unfortunately, this passage is notoriously ambiguous.

> **We groan, longing to be clothed with our heavenly dwelling, because when we are clothed, we will not be found naked. For while we are in this tent, we groan and are burdened, because we do not wish to be unclothed but to be clothed with our heavenly dwelling, so that what is mortal may be swallowed up by life.**

Again at the risk of gross over-simplification, let us examine two basic ways of interpreting these verses that have been adopted.

The traditional line invokes the doctrine of what is sometimes called the 'intermediate state' – that is, there is an interval between a Christian's death and his resurrection at the return of Christ, and in that interval he exists in a state of bliss, as a disembodied spirit. Only at the end of the world does the intermediate state come to an end and the Christian receive the spiritual body of which Paul speaks.

On that interpretation, Paul in verses 2-4 is saying that he has a decided preference for surviving until the return of Christ, rather than dying first; that he would much rather not have to experience the intermediate state because such a 'disembodied nakedness' (which is the phrase he uses) does not appeal to him. Much better to go straight from having an earthly body to having a spiritual one, so that his mortality will simply be swallowed up by the life of the new age.

That interpretation makes quite good sense of the passage but it has limitations. For example, that awkward present tense in verse 1 – 'We have', not 'we will have', a building from God. Paul seems by this to be suggesting that his spiritual body is already in his possession, like a new suit hanging up in the heavenly wardrobe. But that does not seem to fit in with the intermediate state. And the two simple alternatives he seems to present in verses 6 and 8 – 'at home in the body' and 'away from the Lord' – how is that reconciled with the intermediate state? For Paul seems to imply that as soon as he departs this life he expects to enter into the permanency and stability of the final state, with no uncomfortable and undesirable interval.

As a result, some scholars today question the traditional doctrine of the intermediate state. They argue that Paul is saying here that if he does die before Christ returns, he will receive his 'house' from heaven immediately with no intermediate state to endure at all. That is why, they say, he uses the present tense in verse 1. It was there, waiting for him. As for the difficult verses 3 and 4 and the desire not to be found naked, in their view Paul is not expressing a preference for avoiding the intermediate state for he did not believe such existed. What he is doing is rebutting an erroneous view of what happens on death that was gaining currency in the Corinthian church.

We know from 1 Corinthians that there was an element in the Corinthian church that was influenced by Greek ideas and consequently had great difficulty in accepting Paul's doctrine of the resurrection body. The Greeks thought of the body as an encumbrance. They could not imagine why Paul would want another; they would be delighted to get rid of their own. So these people subtly reinterpreted the Christian message, arguing for a purely spiritual resurrection. We find quite clear evidence of this in 1 Corinthians 15. They were trying, one might say, to replace the biblical doctrine of the resurrection of the body with a platonic, philosophical doctrine of the immortality of the soul.

According to that interpretation, Paul's wish to avoid being unclothed has nothing to do with an intermediate state. He is saying, 'As a Christian, this Greek idea of existing in some disembodied soul, with which you Corinthians are flirting at the moment, is quite foreign and repugnant to me; I have no desire for that kind of thing. It is not Christian.' Only an embodied eternal state would do for Paul, and that is what he anticipated he would enjoy the moment he died. For him to be away from the mortal body was to be at home with the Lord in his new spiritual body.

There, very briefly, is the controversy. We need to know about it, but it is not easy to sort out. Indeed, some people claim that even Paul himself had not entirely sorted it out, and that that is why he is somewhat confusing on the subject. For myself, I am increasingly inclined to agree with the second view, as does Murray Harris in a book called *Raised Immortal*,[1] which I recommend if you wish to study the matter further.

My reason for agreeing with those who dispense with the idea of an intermediate state is not just that it makes better sense of 2 Corinthians 5:2-4, though I think it probably does. It is also more consistent with the general flow of Paul's argument right through our study passage in this chapter. Do you remember Paul's argument in 4:16-18? For Paul, resurrection was not merely something in the future. It was a present experience. He thought of Christian existence now as existing in two dimensions simultaneously – this world and the world to come. And those two worlds were not just linked consecutively, they also existed parallel to each other, rather

---

1. *Raised Immortal*, Published by Marshall, Morgan and Scott, 1983

like the parallel universes imagined by science fiction writers. Paul says that a Christian has an identity in each of these parallel worlds, right now.

That, I think, is why he goes straight on to say that we *have* a building from God eternal in the heavens. Of course we have it now, because we already exist in that other world now. 'You have been raised with Christ ... your life is now hidden with Christ in God' (Col. 3:1-3). That was how Paul thought about the matter. When Christ appears it is not a case of being given a new life, but rather that the resurrection life that we already have is going to come out of hiding and appear with Christ in glory.

And that is why Paul goes on to add verse 5:

> Now it is God who has made us for this very purpose and has given us the Spirit as a deposit, guaranteeing what is to come.

Notice that past tense. The life of the new age is something for which a Christian is already made and prepared. And the Holy Spirit is nothing less than the life of that new world, present now in the believer's experience, as a kind of first instalment or foretaste of that new age to come.

(c) Confidence in the face of death

Whether you agree with me in accepting that interpretation or whether you stay with the more traditional one, the practical thrust of what Paul is saying is not greatly affected. So let us turn to that now.

> Therefore we are always confident and know that as long as we are at home in the body we are away from the Lord. We live by faith, not by sight. We are confident, I say, and would prefer to be away from the body and at home with the Lord (5:6-8).

Notice that Paul repeats the phrase 'we are confident'. When it comes to thinking about your own funeral, confidence is a very desirable word; but it is not one that comes very readily to people's lips.

Earlier I asked you how you felt about growing old. Let me now ask you an even bolder question.

How do you feel about dying?

Am I not speaking the truth when I say that for all our twentieth-century sophistication, people are as scared of dying today as they have ever been – probably more so? It is not just the old for whom the fear of death is a problem. Increasingly the prospect of death hangs like a black curtain over the young, too. A student at the Sorbonne in Paris stood up during the Paris riots in the 1960s and said something like this: 'What is my life? I am here to study. In a few years I shall pass my exams. Then I shall go and get a job. I shall make money and get married.' Then he shrugged his shoulders and said, 'What's the point of it all? And the sad thing is, when I'm 40 I'll think it's wonderful! '

What *is* the point of it? If it all ends in a wooden box two metres long, why bother? This is the real dilemma of death. It is not the weakness and the pain that may be its prelude. After all, some people die suddenly without any illness or infirmity to trouble their last years, and there is always hope it will be that way for us too. No. The real dilemma of death is the impenetrable shadow of meaningless-ness that it casts over our whole life. Existence that ends in death is pointless. But ironically we perceive that pointlessness more clearly at 20 than we do at 40.

That is why we muffle death up in that conspiracy of silence; why nobody would talk to that terminal patient in the poem with which this chapter began. Because the moment we face up to the reality of death, we face up to the ultimate insignificance of our lives. We face up to the fact that the tenderest memories we have, the greatest actions we perform, the greatest achievements we have made, every letter after our names, all the love in our hearts, will one day all be erased, and become extinct. No wonder the New Testament speaks of death as a bondage that extends over a man's whole lifetime! Everything is pointless, unless it lasts; but death means that nothing lasts. And for all that we can do with medicine and science, while death remains unconquered man is still the helpless victim of his fate. But not Paul.

No, says Paul, we are confident! Why? Because we know that 'the one who raised the Lord Jesus from the dead will also raise us with Jesus'. Because we know that 'if the earthly tent we live in is destroyed, we have a building from God, an eternal house in the heavens'. Oh, it is true, we cannot yet see this new world of resurrection glory with our physical eyes; we walk by faith, not by sight. But that Christian faith of ours is no vague wishful thinking or pious superstition. We have the empty tomb on our side. We have the eyewitnesses on our side. We have the first instalment of the Holy Spirit on our side.

So this faith we live by is a sanguine, buoyant, confident faith. We do not lose heart, says Paul, even though we are mere clay pots battered and cracked by circumstances, even though outwardly our bodies are growing older and more decrepit every day, for the resurrection life of Jesus has been planted deep within us. Already he is renewing our hearts and minds, already the image of God is being rehabilitated within us by the Spirit's transforming work, already we have a spiritual identity in the new world that is secretly growing and developing even while our mortal nature is growing ever more frail. And one day that spiritual identity is going to swallow up the old nature altogether, so that we who have born the likeness of the man of earth – Adam – will bear the likeness of the man from heaven, Jesus.

People who believe that can be confident. We do not need to be afraid to die. People who believe that can look death in the face with a steady eye. They can even 'go gentle into that good night'. They have no need to 'rage, rage against the dying of the light'. I do not know of any Christian testimony more convincing than that of a man or woman who is able to accept death. As Paul tells us, it is simply moving house; from being at home in the body, we go to be at home with the Lord. Death is as simple and as non-intimidating for the Christian as that.

Daniel Niles tells the story of some missionaries who laboured long and hard among the members of an African tribe, until eventually just one family in this tribe became Christians. Shortly afterwards the eldest son of that family fell seriously ill. The parents and the missionaries prayed for the child's recovery; they longed desperately for a healing to prove to the superstitious tribesmen that God was real. But all their efforts of prayer and medicine failed. The boy died. 'Surely,' they said, 'this is the end of our work. They are never going to believe us now.' But to their amazement, the Chief of the tribe came to them and said, 'We want to become Christians too.'

The missionaries were startled. 'Why?'

'We want to have a God who can make us strong to face death,' replied the Chief, 'the way you and that boy faced it.'

Forgive me if I speak candidly on this matter. Some people by their obsession with physical healing seem to me to rob Christian souls of their privilege and opportunity to glorify God in the way they die. Instead of a triumphant acceptance of death, as simply one more step in the purpose of God for them, we find instead a hysterical search for healing as if it were quite impossible that it should be God's will for a Christian to die. Instead of courageous testimony, we find an attitude towards death that resembles in many ways that cowardly conspiracy of silence and double-think that we find in the world.

It ought not to be so. We Christians are special not because we are immune to death, but because we know what happens when we die. Just as a linguist can translate a word from one language to another yet retain the meaning; just as a musician can transpose a sequence of notes from one key to another yet retain the melody; just as a chemist can transform a substance from one phase to another, yet retain its composition – so we believe God can translate our human existence out of this old world of sin and death into his new world of resurrection life and retain our human identity. We shall be different in that world, radically different, because we shall be like Christ; yet we shall also be the same, radically the same, for we shall never have been more truly ourselves.

Do not begrudge the Christian his grave, then. You who are bereaved, you do not have to mourn without hope. You who are old, you do not have to die without peace. You who are young, you do not have to live without purpose. 'We know that the one who raised the Lord Jesus from the dead will also raise us.'

I do not know of any sentence in the whole Bible more revolutionary than that.

6

Why be an Evangelist?
(2 Corinthians 5:9-6:2)

So we make it our goal to please him, whether we are at home in the body or away from it. For we must all appear before the judgment seat of Christ, that each one may receive what is due him for the things done while in the body, whether good or bad.

Since, then, we know what it is to fear the Lord, we try to persuade men. What we are is plain to God, and I hope it is also plain to your conscience. We are not trying to commend ourselves to you again, but are giving you an opportunity to take pride in us, so that you can answer those who take pride in what is seen rather than what is in the heart. If we are out of our mind, it is for the sake of God; if we are in our right mind, it is for you. For Christ's love compels us, because we are convinced that one died for all, and therefore all died. And he died for all, that those who live should no longer live for themselves but for him who died for them and was raised again.

So from now on we regard no one from a worldly point of view. Though we once regarded Christ in this way, we do so no longer. Therefore, if anyone is in Christ, he is a new creation; the old has gone, the new has come! All this is from God, who reconciled us to himself through Christ and gave us the ministry of reconciliation: that God was reconciling the world to himself in Christ, not counting men's sins against them. And he has committed to us the message of reconciliation. We are therefore Christ's ambassadors, as though God were making his appeal through us. We implore you on Christ's behalf: Be reconciled to God. God made him who had no sin to be sin for us, so that in him we might become the righteousness of God.

As God's fellow workers we urge you not to receive God's grace in vain. For he says,

"In the time of my favour I heard you,
and in the day of salvation I helped you."

I tell you, now is the time of God's favour, now is the day of salvation (2 Corinthians 5:9-6:2).

108

THE SEA OF GALILEE AND THE DEAD SEA ARE BOTH LAND-LOCKED LAKES. But there is a significant difference between them. The Sea of Galilee has both an inlet and an outlet; it is, as it were, a comma on the long neck of the River Jordan. Water flowing south pauses there before moving on, and as a result the Sea of Galilee is alive with fish. But the Dead Sea only has an inlet; it is a 'full stop' in the River Jordan. None of its water ever finds its way out into the ocean, and the result is that the Dead Sea is lifeless, with such a high concentration of dissolved minerals in it that it is not even fit to drink. All of which is quite a thought-provoking parable of the Christian church.

A Christianity that only has 'in-pipes' is going to be a dead Christianity. No matter how much sound teaching we hear, no matter how much warm fellowship we enjoy, no matter how much pastoral care we receive, no matter how much theological literature we read – if it does not flow out in Christian witness to the world at large then all that we take in, far from benefiting us spiritually, will just serve to increase our spiritual sterility. We will be like a reservoir without any taps to supply, generators to turn or rivers to feed. We will just grow more and more stale and unwholesome.

Do you want to know how to kill a church? Fasten its members' attention purely on internal matters. Get them agitated about what hymn book they should sing from. Make them anxious about charismatic enthusiasm in their midst, or about the sins of the ecumenical movement. Get them totally absorbed in a new building programme, or in fund-raising activities, or in simply being nosy about one another's problems. It does not really matter what the issue is, so long as it has the effect of drying up their outreach. Then stand back and wait for spiritual gangrene to set in and do its lethal work. Go back a generation or two later and you will find that church has become one of those nasty cliques that are dominated by a handful of inter-bred families who cannot give up the habit of chapel-going. The church will have been murdered. To be more precise, it will have committed suicide. If such a church remains orthodox, it is a dead orthodoxy; if it retains a congregation, it is a lifeless congregation. As often as not, of course, they do neither.

They simply disappear, leaving their once-busy chapels to be turned into factories or mosques.

A Bible college in this country used to have for its motto, 'Evangelise or Perish'. A trifle over-dramatic, perhaps, but basically true: the key to any church's life is its evangelism. Expect poison in standing water.

For most of us, this is probably old news. Most of us know that Christians ought to be taking God's word out into the world, and many of us feel guilt-ridden about our failure to do so.

Our problem is how to prime the pump to get the water flowing. The motivation is not there. Maybe it is our natural shyness or our British reserve; maybe it is our preoccupation with other things. Whatever the reason, many of us if we were honest would have to admit that we can go from one month's – even year's – end to the other, and never speak to anybody about the good news which once we were so glad somebody told us.

So where are we going to find the vitality that will change us from being a dead sea into being a living river? Where are we going to find the incentive to make our church, instead of one that takes in much and gives out little, a church which passes on the water of life it receives and as a result teems with fertility?

The passage we shall be studying in this chapter will help us considerably with these questions, if we allow it to. For in this passage Paul, who I think we must consider one of the most outgoing Christians of all time, is telling us what motivated his missionary endeavour: he is answering the question, 'Why be an evangelist?'.

1. The verdict of the judge (5:9-11)

> So we make it our goal to please him, whether we are at home in the body or away from it. For we must all appear before the judgment seat of Christ, that each one may receive what is due to him for the things done while in the body, whether good or bad. Since, then, we know what it is to fear the Lord, we try to persuade men (5:9-11).

I suspect that one of the complaints that Paul's rivals had about his evangelistic style was that it was too blunt and confrontational. 'That Paul!' they were saying. 'He presses Christianity on people too obviously. There's no subtlety, no sophistication about his marketing techniques; he needs to go on a soft-sell training course. As it is, he puts off more people than he attracts. He has no discretion, no finesse!' To use the word which I suspect they used (and which Paul mimics in verse 11), 'he *persuades* people', they said – the Greek word sometimes has a pejorative tone; it can mean 'cajoling', 'bullying' or 'browbeating'. And Paul in these verses says, 'Maybe it is true; maybe I do "persuade" people as you put it. But there is a reason for my uncompromising forthrightness. We must all appear before the judgment seat of Christ. Since then we know what it is to fear the Lord, we try to persuade men.'

This is Paul's first motivation for evangelism. He was painfully aware of the ultimate accountability of the whole human race to Christ the judge. A verdict was going to be delivered. The resurrection of Jesus had made the issue of death largely irrelevant for Paul – whether he was at home in the body or at home with the Lord – but it had made the issue of final judgment all the more pressing. It was not going through the valley of the shadow of death that bothered him, but facing the assize that awaited him on the far side of that valley. 'For we must all appear before the judgment seat of Christ.'

Do you not find that a solemn thought? Notice some things about it.

First, the *individuality* of this judgment. Each one may receive what is due him, says Paul. We are not then going to be assessed as societies, or as churches, or even as families. We stand alone before the judge to bear the consequences of our own personal responsibility, each one of us. It's said that President Truman kept a little notice on his desk: 'The buck stops here'. There can be no excuses, no passing the blame, says Paul, One day you will have to stand under judgment, and you will have to stand there by yourself.

Second, the *visibility* of it. We are going to 'appear' before the judgment seat of Christ. It was the usual word in Greek, as in

English, for a public indictment in court. But I think it had added significance for Paul because he uses the word often in these chapters when speaking of the openness of his preaching method and leadership style. He used it again in verse 11: 'What we are is plain to God, and I hope it is also plain to your conscience.' He knew that one day there would be no more secrecy, sham, hypocrisy, ulterior motives or skeletons in the cupboard; they would all be exposed. If he was not open with people now, he would have to be then. There would be no cover-ups, no private confessionals. To use a metaphor of Jesus, things that had been whispered in secret would be shouted from the housetops.

Third, the *impartiality* of it. 'Each one may receive what is due to him for the things done while in the body, whether good or bad.' Some people find that difficult, because of Paul's doctrine of justification by faith: surely Paul is suggesting here that salvation is by good works – the very thing he denies so emphatically in other writings, like the letter to the Romans? Indeed, some are so anxious to avoid the embarrassment of that, that they theorise there will actually be two judgments: one conducted by God to settle people's destiny on the basis of faith, and the other conducted by Christ to decide the rewards that Christians will receive based on works.

I suspect that this is hair-splitting that Paul would not have accepted. Of course he believed that people must be saved through faith, not works. He says so repeatedly. But it is quite wrong to conclude that Paul believed that good works were unnecessary to Christian living. On the contrary, he believed most firmly that good works were indispensable as evidence of our salvation. That is why he was able to say to the Galatians, 'Don't let anybody fool you. If you practise the works of the flesh you are not going to inherit the kingdom of heaven' (cf. Gal. 6:7-8). It is as simple as that. He did not imagine that God would, on the last day, have to ask men and women whether they were believers; that would be transparently obvious when the books were opened and their lives were revealed. So it will be an impartial judgment. Christ will observe the differences between individuals, and separate them as sheep from goats.

But fourth, and most important, I want you to notice the *universality* of this judgment. We must 'all' appear, Paul included.

Some find difficulty with that, too. What has become of Paul's assurance? Did he seriously believe that as a Christian, he was in danger of being condemned? I do not believe he did. But, it is clear from this verse, neither did he believe that a Christian ought to be complacent about final judgment. To be justified by faith is not the same thing as to be immune from criticism. Paul was still responsible for what he did with his life, and he expected to give an account of that life. He did not relish the prospect of having to stand before his Master, blushing and ashamed.

(a) A verdict that adds urgency to the task
The judgment seat of Christ is not meant, then, to cloud our Christian assurance but it is a spur to our Christian commitment. That is exactly what it was for Paul. 'Since ... we know what it is to fear the Lord,' he says, 'we try to persuade men.' How can he be anything but forthright in his evangelism, when he knows that he has to appear before the judgment seat of Christ? How can he face Jesus with a clear conscience if he knows he has neglected the task of sharing the gospel with men and women who must stand there too? I suggest that if, like Paul, we lived with the flavour of judgment in our mouth, we would undoubtedly be less reserved and less laid-back about our evangelism. The verdict of the judge adds urgency to the task. As Paul expresses it in his second letter to Timothy: 'In the presence of God and of Christ Jesus, who will judge the living and the dead, and in view of his appearing and his kingdom, I give you this charge: Preach the Word ...' (2 Tim. 4:1-2). Preach the word whether the occasion is convenient or inconvenient to you or to your hearers; do the work of an evangelist, Paul says. People do not have forever to repent. Must we smell hell before we realise that the plight of unconverted men and women is formidably serious?

(b) A verdict that adds integrity to the evangelist's character

'What we are is plain to God, and I hope it is also plain to your conscience.' Paul simply could not go along with the underhanded manipulative techniques that his rivals were recommending. Maybe he lacked subtlety and sophistication; maybe he sometimes put people off by the way he spoke. But when it came to the final judgment it was not his sales figures that were going to be assessed but his sales methods. 'I must be frank and open with people,' says Paul. 'I must lay it on the line for them. I cannot keep the gospel wrapped up in a seductive cloak of tantalising mystery even if such tactics would win more adherents. God is going to judge me. I would rather stand before him with a clear conscience and be accused of being a bit tactless on occasions, than bear the awful shame of being a mere peddler of the gospel who distorts the word of God for the sake of popularity.'

Imagine you knew that tomorrow the clocks would stop, that tomorrow would be the day when time would come to an end, the books of judgment would be opened and all human beings would face their Maker. Would there not be some telephone calls you would want to make today? Some telegrams you would want to send? Some visits you would want to make?

Evangelism is not a Christian hobby. It is a rescue operation, as urgent as any lifeboat that goes out into a gale-swept sea. The verdict of the judge leaves us with no option but to start carving outlets from the Dead Sea of our sterile introversion.

2. The love of the Saviour (5:12-17)

> If we are out of our mind, it is for the sake of God; if we are in our right mind, it is for you. For Christ's love compels us (5:13-14).

We have already seen that Paul was not really concerned to vindicate his reputation for his own sake; in fact he felt embarrassed to speak in what seem a self-congratulatory fashion. The only reason he was writing in this defensive way was for the sake of those who were loyal to him at Corinth, as he puts it in verse 12: 'We ... are giving you an opportunity to take pride in us, so that you can answer' those who are finding fault with me!

Now in verses 13 and 14 he explains why he is able to be so detached from the criticisms that were being levelled against him. Quite simply, his ego was not at stake. He could not care less what people thought of his preaching. His experience of Christ had put him beyond self-centred considerations. 'Christ's love compels us, because we are convinced that one died for all, and therefore all died. And he died for all, that those who live should no longer live for themselves' – that is the key phrase – 'but for him who died for them and was raised again' (verses 14-15). The love of Christ means that I am free from egocentricity, says Paul. My self-esteem is no longer bound up with what people think of me or my preaching.

It is not easy, it must be admitted, to see how verse 13 fits in with that general line of thought: 'If we are out of our mind, it is for the sake of God; if we are in our right mind, it is for you.' The sentence can be taken in two ways. One way is to understand Paul to be referring to the polarised reactions that his preaching evoked in people. Some people admired the sharpness of his intellect: others, like Festus in the book of Acts, concluded that much learning had driven him crazy! If that is Paul's meaning then he is saying that he does not care what people say: if they accuse him of fanaticism he is glad, because he is 'out of his mind' for God's sake, and will gladly bear the stigma of insanity for him. And if people admire him for being such a great intellectual, then he is glad too; it means that the Corinthians can boast that they have an academically respectable advocate on their side. But as far as Paul is concerned, it makes no difference either way. The love of Christ has rendered him indifferent both to the flattery and the criticism of human beings.

That may very well be what Paul means. But there is an alternative explanation of verse 13. Paul could be referring to one of the accusations made by his rivals. It may be that they found Paul's style of rational argument in preaching uncongenial. Perhaps they wanted

more evidence of mystical rapture, of inspired rhetoric, of supernatural charisma. That is quite possible, because we know from
Paul's first letter to the Corinthians that the church there was very
enamoured with supernatural gifts of utterance such as tongues. It
may be that Paul's preaching style was regarded by some of those
Corinthian enthusiasts as too prosaic. If that is the sense, then what
Paul is saying is: 'Look, I do have my moments of spiritual ecstasy
when I am "out of my mind". But they are private, between me and
God. I do not put such divine intoxication on public display; it will
only draw attention to me, and that is not what preaching is all about.
No, when I preach I preach rationally and coherently, and I do so for
your sake, so that you will understand the message I bring and will
not fall in love with me – Paul, the great preacher and orator; but will
fall in love with the Saviour who is at the heart of the message I
bring. The love of Christ controls the style and delivery of my
preaching.'

It is not easy to choose between the two alternatives, though the
more I understand of the nature of Paul's Corinthian opponents, the
more inclined I am to prefer the second. But either way, the central
point that Paul is making is not in question. He is telling us that the
pivot of all his aspirations is no longer his own reputation. He is not
the centre of his universe any more. He lives for Christ, whose glory
is the determining factor in all his thinking. Why? Because Christ
died for him. As far as Paul is concerned, the sacrifice that Jesus
made on the cross means the death of the old Paul, with his obsessive
self-righteousness and over-weening pride. He can no longer live
for himself in that way. God has put to death that old man, and given
him a whole new focus for living. 'I live no longer for myself but for
him,' he says. Indeed he wishes that were true for everybody; Christ
did not die only for him but as a representative of the whole human
race. He died for all.

'And that is why I must be an evangelist, don't you see?' says
Paul. 'The love of Christ for me and for all men compels me in this
matter.'

Is not that a challenging thought? If we are honest, we must admit that many of our inhibitions about evangelism derive from our self-consciousness. 'What will he think of me if I tell him I am a Christian?' 'What will she say about me behind my back if I offer to read the Bible with her?' We are so concerned about our self-esteem, so desperate that the gospel should not cost us our reputation among our friends and neighbours. Whenever Paul was tempted to think like that, he turned his mind to the cross. 'You are not on this planet to live for yourself any longer,' he told himself. 'Christ has died for you, you have no right to live for anyone else but him.'

How much more unrestrained we would be in our personal witness, if we thought like that!

Paul now develops this thought of the constraining love of Christ a little further.

> So from now on we regard no-one from a worldly point of view. Though we once regarded Christ in this way, we do so no longer. Therefore, if anyone is in Christ, he is a new creation; the old has gone, the new has come! (5:16-17).

Once again, there is a small area of debate about these verses. What exactly does Paul mean when he says, 'We once regarded Christ from a worldly point of view but we do so no longer'?

Some modern scholars have pressed this verse to mean that Paul drew a complete line of distinction between the Jesus of history – the real Jesus who walked this earth – and the Christ of Paul's spiritual experience. They say that Paul is saying here that really he was only interested in the latter; that he was not at all bothered about the Jesus of history, only in the Jesus he knew in his own personal experience through faith.

I do not think that is true. Paul was profoundly concerned about the historical reliability of the central gospel events, and particularly the death and resurrection of Jesus. In 1 Corinthians 15 he goes out of his way to establish the historicity of the resurrection in the face of false teaching that wanted to remove the resurrection from the realm of history and spiritualise it, in exactly the way that these scholars suggest. So it is quite nonsensical to think that when Paul says 'I once knew Jesus from a worldly point of view, and now I do not see him that way any longer' that he means 'I used to think about Jesus as a person of history, now I regard him as a myth.'

A more plausible theory is that Paul is confessing that he once entertained false ideas of Messiahship: that he thought of the kingdom of Christ as materialistic or even militaristic. Many Jews thought that in the first century. If that is the case, then he is saying that he realises now that the Messianic kingdom was not about a new, independent state of Israel (that is, 'a worldly point of view'); no, Christ is about a new creation in the hearts of men and women generally, Jew and Gentile.

Yet it may be that the simplest explanation of these verses is, in fact, the right one; namely that Paul is saying, 'Look, once upon a time I saw Jesus in purely human terms. I thought of him as a dangerous rabbi teaching seditious ideas to my people; so I perse-cuted him. But now I realise I was wrong, for my eyes have been opened to see the real Jesus, the divine glory that was veiled in his flesh.' That knowledge of Jesus, he says, is the important one. After all, many people knew Jesus on a human level and derived no benefit at all from his acquaintance. The vital thing is not to be able to answer a GCSE question on the gospel narratives, but to experi-ence a personal encounter with the divine Jesus to whom those gospel narratives witness.

It would of course have been a particularly relevant point if one of the things that Paul's rivals were saying about him was that he was disqualified from apostleship because he did not know Jesus before the resurrection. 'He is not one of the Twelve; so what sort of apostle is he?' It could well be that they tried to undermine Paul in just that way.

But once again, which ever way you read the passage, Paul's central thought in these verses is clear. Coming to recognise who Jesus really is has not only changed the way Paul views him, but it has changed the way he looks at people generally. 'From now on we regard no-one from a worldly point of view ... If any one is in Christ, he is a new creation.'

It is a wonderful thought. Paul is saying he no longer saw people around him from the pessimistic perspective of this sinful world. In a sense, he did not see people as they were but as the transformed personalities they could become: if only, like him, they discovered who Jesus really was, and participated with him in the powers of the age to come. 'A new creation' he says, and there is an air of wonder and amazement in the Greek. Becoming a Christian is like waking up out of a dream. You blink, and behold – the old has disappeared. Everything is new. You feel rather as Noah must have felt when he came out of the ark and saw a new world stretching before him. 'This is what the love of Christ does for me. It not only strips the egotism from my heart, it drives me out in a passionate desire that other men and women should discover this new beginning in Christ that I have found.'

Should not that motivate us, too? Should not the love of Christ transform our perspective on people around us, as we see what they could become if Christ entered their lives?

God save us from evangelism that is not empowered with that kind of love for people! God save us from evangelical scalp-hunting, the evangelism that showers the world with lurid tracts proclaiming that 'God loves you', but which fails to show one glimmer of that costly involvement with human beings which is what love is all about. God forgive us for those Christian trophy-hunters who stalk converts all day and spend their nights totting up their 'kills' in little notebooks.

How much we need the love of Christ controlling and constraining us in our evangelism! How much damage we will do, if it isn't!

That was Paul's second great motivation, and even if it were the only one, I believe it ought to be enough. But he has a third.

3. The commission of the king (5:18-6:2)

All this is from God, who reconciled us to himself through Christ and gave us the ministry of reconciliation: that God was reconciling the world to himself in Christ, not counting men's sins against them. And he has committed to us the message of reconciliation. We are therefore Christ's ambassadors, as though God were making his appeal through us. We implore you on Christ's behalf: Be reconciled to God. God made him who had no sin to be sin for us, so that in him we might become the righteousness of God.

As God's fellow workers we urge you not to receive God's grace in vain. For he says,

> **"In the time of my favour I heard you,**
> **and in the day of salvation I helped you."**

I tell you, now is the time of God's favour, now is the day of salvation (5:18-6:2).

You will not find the portfolio of 'the ministry of reconciliation' in any Cabinet office, but it is entrusted to us. We have seen how the prospect of judgment to come moved Paul to be an evangelist. We have seen how his experience of the love of Christ encouraged him in the same direction. But of course, the chief reason that Paul was a preacher of the gospel was not because he felt he ought to be one, but because God had called him to undertake such a task.

These verses that follow on from verse 18 are so important and so rich that we could easily have devoted the whole of this chapter to them. Paul is outlining here the entire core of the gospel message that he was commissioned to preach. It is, he says, a message about *a great act of divine initiative*: 'All this is from God': Christianity then is not about human beings finding their way to God, it is about God sovereignly making a way to himself by a gigantic act of condescension. Secondly, the message contains *a great act of divine acquittal*: 'God was reconciling the world to himself in Christ, not counting men's sins against them.' This is the root problem that Christianity addresses. Not the ignorance of men, though men without Christ are ignorant; not the meaninglessness of life, though life without Christ is meaningless; it is the guilt of the human race which is the primary obstacle between man and God, says Paul. We need to be reconciled to God because our moral failure, our sin, has alienated us from him and it is that moral failure that God was determined to overcome – and he did overcome in Christ. Thirdly, the message contains *a great act of divine substitution*: 'God made him who had no sin to be sin for us, so that in him we might become the righteousness of God.'

Do you notice the beautiful symmetry of that verse? Paul is describing a great exchange: on one side there is Christ who is sinless, on the other side, there is man who is sinful. As a result of God's gracious intervention, what happens? Christ is made sin, and man becomes righteous. So simple, and yet, when you think about it, so extraordinarily wonderful! What other word could describe what Paul is saying here, except *substitution*? It becomes transparently clear now what Paul meant when he said earlier in verse 15 that Christ died *for* men and women. Paul does not mean that Christ died just to set us all an example of self-sacrificial love. He means he died 'instead' of men and women. He took their guilt upon himself and bore the penalty for it. He was their substitute.

Some people object to such an interpretation of the cross. They say that it is morally scandalous to imagine God punishing an innocent third party for other people's sins. What they overlook is the fact that according to Paul's gospel, Jesus, though innocent, was not a third party. In fact, verse 19 can and should be translated in such a way as to make that quite explicit: 'God was *in Christ*, reconciling the world to himself.' God and Christ are not two parties as far as this exchange is concerned. They are one. God was not laying the sins of the world upon somebody else when he placed them on Christ. He was placing the sin of the world on himself.

What we see on the cross is all the outrage, indignation, anger and pain that the sin of the world causes a holy God; and we see that pain and that anger being inflicted, not on those who deserve it (ourselves) but being absorbed instead by an internal agony within the Godhead. God was *in Christ* reconciling the world to himself; that is why the blood which was shed on the cross can rightly be called the blood of God. And that is why the love which was shown on the cross can rightly be called the love of God. It was God who was doing the loving, when in Christ he reconciled the world to himself.

These are stupendous truths. They are condensed by Paul into such an economy of words: but any theologian worth his salt would have no difficulty in writing an entire book if not an entire library of exposition on the doctrine Paul is teaching. And yet it is not this great act of divine initiative, and it is not this great act of divine acquittal, and it is not this great act of divine substitution, to which I chiefly want to draw your attention; because none of these is in fact the central point Paul wishes to make. He is commenting on these things almost as an aside.

Paul's chief subject in these verses is *the great act of divine delegation* which issued out of this salvation of which he speaks. He mentions it three times. In verse 18: 'God gave us the ministry of reconciliation.' In verse 19: 'He committed to us the message of reconciliation.' In verse 20: 'We are therefore Christ's ambassadors, as though God were making his appeal through us. We implore you on Christ's behalf: Be reconciled to God.' It is astonishing that the publicity of this great plan of cosmic reconciliation, all devised and executed by God himself, is not placed in God's own hands, not even in the hands of angels, but in our hands!

Notice three things about this privileged ministry.

First, Paul's emphasis on the *message* of reconciliation. That is important, for it implies that evangelism requires more than silent testimony; it requires words. It is, at root, an act of communication; the message about what God has done in Christ has to be passed on. Certainly people will be encouraged to listen as a result of our Christian behaviour, and the message will be received with more plausibility when it is heard in the context of a community that demonstrates the love of Christ. But we cannot hide behind the silent witness of our lives. No one can believe the gospel unless they have *heard* it. Faith comes by *hearing*; therefore we cannot be evangelists unless we open our mouths.

Second, the *dignity* of this work, as Paul describes it. We are Christ's 'ambassadors'. People sometimes ask me what right we have to intrude upon the lives of other people with the gospel: 'It's so impolite, so un-British!' If that is your problem, you are forgetting that an evangelist is not some interfering busybody, but a personal representative of the King of kings. No doubt such an office requires of us diplomacy, but it also bestows upon us dignity. We have every right to face men and women with the claims of Jesus Christ. He is their rightful sovereign, whether they acknowledge him or not.

But notice, third, the *solemnity* of this work of evangelism. 'We implore you on Christ's behalf: Be reconciled to God.' Reconciliation is a two-sided business. The message of the cross is that God has reconciled the world to himself, but the agony of the evangelist is that there are many in that world who have not yet been reconciled to God. In spite of his great act of initiative, in spite of his great act of acquittal, in spite of his extraordinary act of substitution on behalf of sinners, they still remain obdurate in their moral rebellion. You can almost feel the heartache in Paul's words: 'We implore you,' he says, 'on Christ's behalf' – as if it were Jesus himself standing before you with nail prints in his hands, and begging you: we are ambassadors of the king and we beg you to accept the reconciliation he so graciously offers you.

If the thought of Christ's judgment throne is not enough to persuade us that we ought to be reaching out to men and women; if the experience of the love of Christ is not sufficient to free us from our self-consciousness and our inhibitions; then does not this great commission which Christ has given to his church, the ministry of reconciliation, place upon us a duty to tell others?

If these three great incentives are not enough to make evangelists of us, then the church will die. It will dry up. And it will deserve to dry up. It is nothing but a salt sea, with inlets and no outlets.

But before we end this chapter, let me address those of my readers who are not Christians. Have you noticed, the word 'all' is used in two different ways in this passage? In verse 10, Paul says, 'We must *all* appear before the judgment seat of Christ'. I assure you, you are included in that 'all'. And I believe that deep down in your heart, you know it; you know intuitively that you are personally responsible for your life and that you will give account to your Maker for it. There is no running away from that 'all'.

But there is a second 'all'. Look at verse 14: 'Christ's love compels us, because we are convinced that one died for *all*.' Now tell me – if you are numbered in the first 'all', why should you not be numbered in that second 'all'? Does the Bible leave you out? Does it say Christ died for all except you?

I am writing now to tell you that you can know that you are numbered in that 'all' for whom Christ died. You say, 'How?' Be reconciled to God: that is Paul's answer. God has reached down from heaven for you. He has sent his Son to bear the sin of this world. What keeps you out of that 'all' for whom Christ died is not God's unwillingness to be your friend, it is your unwillingness to be his friend! Do you not see? There is no barrier to you becoming a Christian at all, except the one in your own heart. It is not that God will not have you, it is that you will not have him.

That is why I am begging you, as Paul begged his hearers: Be reconciled to God. Stop living for yourself and start living for the Jesus who died for you. And do it today, now. You may say, 'Why – what's the hurry?' Paul tells you why, in his closing verses:

> **As God's fellow workers we urge you not to receive God's grace in vain. For he says,**
>
> > **"In the time of my favour I heard you, and in the day of salvation I helped you."**
>
> **I tell you, now is the time of God's favour, now is the day of salvation** (6:1-2).

This invitation to give up your enmity and become God's friend, this great amnesty that heaven has declared, is extended to you in this critical moment of history, today. But it will not be so extended indefinitely. There is a time limit. *Now* is the time of God's favour, *now* is the time of salvation, says the apostle.

You may say, 'What about tomorrow, then?'

But, you see, that takes us back to the place where we began. Tomorrow we must all appear before the judgment seat of Christ. That is why it has to be today.

7

Living as the Gospel Demands
(2 Corinthians 6:3-7:1)

We put no stumbling block in anyone's path, so that our ministry will not be discredited. Rather, as servants of God we commend ourselves in every way: in great endurance; in troubles, hardships and distresses; in beatings, imprisonments and riots; in hard work, sleepless nights and hunger; in purity, understanding, patience and kindness; in the Holy Spirit and in sincere love; in truthful speech and in the power of God; with weapons of righteousness in the right hand and in the left; through glory and dishonour, bad report and good report; genuine, yet regarded as impostors; known, yet regarded as unknown; dying, and yet we live on; beaten, and yet not killed; sorrowful, yet always rejoicing; poor, yet making many rich; having nothing, and yet possessing everything.

We have spoken freely to you, Corinthians, and opened wide our hearts to you. We are not withholding our affection from you, but you are withholding yours from us. As a fair exchange - I speak as to my children - open wide your hearts also.

Do not be yoked together with unbelievers. For what do righteousness and wickedness have in common? Or what fellowship can light have with darkness? What harmony is there between Christ and Belial? What does a believer have in common with an unbeliever? What agreement is there between the temple of God and idols? For we are the temple of the living God. As God has said: "I will live with them and walk among them, and I will be their God, and they will be my people."

"Therefore come out from them
and be separate,

says the Lord.

Touch no unclean thing,
and I will receive you."
"I will be a Father to you,
and you will be my sons and daughters,

says the Lord Almighty."

Since we have these promises, dear friends, let us purify ourselves from everything that contaminates body and spirit, perfecting holiness out of reverence for God (2 Corinthians 6:3-7:1).

'WHY BE TRAPPED IN A DATSUN, WHEN YOU'VE GOT A DAIMLER FAITH?'

My friend had underlined the slogan in an article he had sent me from a Christian magazine, feeling no doubt that it was peculiarly appropriate to me. He knows that I drive a Datsun and has probably observed that being six feet five inches tall, I do feel rather trapped in the limited leg room which its Japanese designers have ordained! A Daimler would be altogether more comfortable, I cannot deny it. But as a Christian, should I expect that God intends to give me such an expensive limousine? Should I pray for it, believing that I will get it? The article in question was decidedly of the opinion that I should! 'God wants every one of his children to prosper,' it told me. 'You are the child of the King who owns the cattle on a thousand hills, so why should you live like a pauper? He has promised to give you whatever you ask for in faith, so just "Name it and claim it!"'

You may recognise that line. The author belongs to a school of prosperity teaching which is becoming very popular in some Christian circles today. The author's photograph, prominently displayed several times in the text, reminded me of those sleek, well-groomed, executive types that pour into the City of London every morning. In small print at the end it informed me that he was pastor of a church in South Africa that had grown to a membership of 8,000 in less than 10 years and had recently erected a £5,000,000 building complex.

My inferiority complex plunged to new depths of ignominy and inadequacy. Why be trapped in a Datsun, when you have got a Daimler faith? – Why indeed, I asked myself; I am going to get down on my knees right now and start praying for a bigger car, a bigger house, a bigger church, a bigger salary, a bigger ... and then I looked down; and beside the magazine on my desk lay my Bible, open at the passage which we come to in this chapter. My eyes fell on the words:

> In troubles, hardships and distresses; in beatings, imprisonments and riots; in hard work, sleepless nights and hunger ... sorrowful, yet always rejoicing; poor, yet making many rich; having nothing, and yet possessing everything (6:4-5,10).

Suddenly my dream of a Daimler dissolved! Well, it was a tissue of fantasy, after all. The spell of 'prosperity doctrine' was broken; I saw it afresh for the sub-Christian seduction that it is. Great men and women of God do not pray for Daimlers; they pray for endurance. Great men and women of God do not seek bigger salaries; they seek holiness. Great men and women of God do not make it their ambition to look like over-fed stockbrokers; they make it their ambition to look like Jesus.

Nowhere is that made clearer in the Bible than in these emotionally-charged verses we come to now. Paul is pressing upon us, by personal example and personal exhortation, that as far as Christianity is concerned it is not we who make demands on God, it is God who makes demands on us. He demands, first of all, that we be utterly committed to Jesus Christ. He demands, secondly, that we become utterly different from the world around us. And the question he puts to us from this passage is quite simply, Are we ready to be thus committed? thus different? Unlike the magazine article, Paul offers no material prosperity as a bribe. If you get a Datsun out of it, you should count yourself as one of the lucky ones! As for Daimlers – they may have more space for your legs, but how much room is there for your cross – that cross which Jesus said we had to take up daily if we wanted to follow him?

Paul rebukes our lack of wholeheartedness. He pleads for a Christianity that is willing to make sacrifices, to endure adversity, to be unpopular, to live as the gospel demands and not as the world suggests. And at the end of our study, I believe every one of us will have responded to that plea. We will have either said, 'Yes, that is the sort of Christianity that interests me, Paul', or we will have said, 'No, no deal, Paul; your price is too high.'

Neutrality is not really an option when one is faced with words as passionate and imperative as these that Paul directs at us here.

1. A willingness to be committed (6:3-10)

We put no stumbling block in anyone's path, so that our ministry will not be discredited. Rather, as servants of God we commend ourselves in every way: in great endurance (6:3-4).

The apostle has been forced on to the defensive by his critics. They have asserted that his leadership style is inappropriate, that as an apostle he is far too unimpressive and that as a preacher he is far too straightforward. For the best part of five chapters he has been explaining, often very movingly, why he exercises the kind of ministry he does. 'If I were to be the kind of preacher these friends of yours want me to be,' he declares, 'I would not be a true apostle of Jesus Christ. I would be just a salesman of cheap religious baubles. There are plenty of peddlers of God's word around, but I am not one of them. I do not present a false image either of myself or of the gospel. I quite simply tell people the truth and commend it to their conscience in the sight of God. We don't put stumbling-blocks in anyone's path,' he says.

If people dislike Paul's preaching, then that is up to them; but let them be clear that it is the content of the Christian message they are rejecting, not his weak presentation of it! Nothing he does, he claims, makes it difficult for people to become Christians: indeed, he takes pains to avoid any possibility of unnecessary offence. People are all too ready to mock the gospel, to use any defect in a preacher's conduct or character as an excuse to dismiss what he says. Paul is determined not to give anybody a chance to do so.

If his critics accuse him of not living up to their expectations of what an apostle ought to be like, his answer is that the gospel does not need their kind of advocate. And if they want to know what really commends a Christian minister as a servant of God, he will tell them: commitment, total commitment to Jesus Christ.

(a) A commitment that breeds perseverance:

> **in great endurance; in troubles, hardships and distresses; in
> beatings, imprisonments and riots; in hard work, sleepless
> nights and hunger...**

Paul acknowledges that he is no Greek hero, no mighty Hercules –
but nobody will see him retreating in cowardice from danger. There
will be no whining complaints from his lips. He has suffered
anguish, torture and deprivation of all kinds, but in all the rigours of
his ministry he sought to demonstrate endurance. His commitment
to Jesus Christ required such perseverance, and he considered that
such perseverance commends his ministry better than any amount
of rhetoric.

(b) A commitment that issues in integrity:

> **in purity, understanding, patience and kindness; in the
> Holy Spirit and in sincere love; in truthful speech and in the
> power of God; with weapons of righteousness in the right
> hand and in the left ...**

'Examine any part of my life,' says Paul. 'In my private life you will
find that I strive for innocence and purity. In my social relationships
you will find I seek to display sensitivity and tolerance. In my
spiritual life you will find the gifts and fruit that indicate God's
presence is there, with no trace of pretence. And as for my preaching
– nobody can deny that my goal is candid honesty about what the
word of God says and total dependence upon divine illumination in
my hearers. There is no sales talk; no audience manipulation; no
false advertising; no propaganda. Just a frank declaration of what
the gospel says, in the expectation that God's power will authenticate it in the hearts and minds of my audience. "In truthful speech
and in the power of God": I have no magician's tricks up my sleeve.
I rely for my credibility on moral character. My commitment to
Jesus Christ requires that of me. "The weapons of righteousness in
the right hand and in the left."

'And I reckon that integrity to be better commendation than any degree in religious studies at the University of Athens.'

(c) A commitment that breeds contentment:

> **through glory and dishonour, bad report and good report; genuine, yet regarded as impostors; known, yet regarded as unknown; dying, and yet we live on; beaten, and yet not killed; sorrowful, yet always rejoicing; poor, yet making many rich; having nothing, and yet possessing everything ...**

Everybody knows that Paul's experience of fame and fortune has oscillated wildly! One moment everybody cheers him, the next moment they are waving their fists at him. One day he is hailed as a great apostle; the next he is scorned as a charlatan. But the applause does not go to his head; the boos do not humiliate him.

'There is a resilience about me,' says Paul, 'which amazes even me: not even material destitution can demoralise me for long, because I can honestly say that my self-esteem is not bound up with my popularity ratings or my salary cheques.' Just as that article said with which we began, Paul knew he was the child of a king who owned the cattle on a thousand hills. But contrary to the article, that knowledge bred in him not a sanctified acquisitiveness but a humble contentment. He just goes on doing the job that God has given him to do. And his reason? He knows that if he does *not* endure adversity manfully; if he is *not* impeccable in his personal behaviour; if he allows failure and disappointment to get him down, then someone will say: 'Ah! Christianity does not work after all! Look at Paul, he's just a lot of hot air.'

Paul is determined that he is not going to be that kind of hindrance to anybody. 'We put no stumbling-block in anyone's path, so that our ministry will not be discredited. Rather, as servants of God we commend ourselves in every way.' There were plenty of magicians, orators, and muscle-men around for the Greek world to hero-worship; but Christian perseverance, integrity and contentment are rare, because they are the fruits of real Christian commitment. And

Christian commitment is something the world can neither imitate nor deny. It is an unimpeachable credential.

Tell me, what is your image of Christianity? Old ladies in hats, perhaps? A Sunday School of six-year-olds singing 'I am H-A-P-P-Y'? A couple of nervous pimply students offering you an invitation to a coffee-party at the college Christian Union? Is that what puts you off Christianity – that it is all too wet and effeminate? Or is it the showy professionalism of mass evangelism that antagonises you – that gleaming transatlantic smile that beams down at you from the video relay, the oily sincerity of the soloist as she croons her gospel entertainment, the unscrupulous emotionalism of the appeal, fanned by humming choirs and tear-stained faces? Is that what turns you off? The mass-evangelistic spectacular with its glossy advertising and its razzmatazz?

Perhaps it is the respectable image of the church that you dislike. Those rows of new cars parked outside each Sunday, those terribly 'nice' people in their 'frightfully chic' outfits you meet inside? The vicar who talks with a plum in his mouth and those delicate cucumber sandwiches his wife offers you at the tea party? Is it all too conventional, too middle-class?

Do not be misled by wimpish Christian caricatures. Do not be put off by examples of Christian showmanship. Do not be deterred by images of Christian affluence. There is plenty of so-called Christianity in this world that is pathetically fashionable, superficially showy, and boringly trite. It turns my stomach, and I do not mind in the least if you tell me it turns yours too. But the existence of a thousand fakes does not mean there is no such thing as a genuine diamond. The Christianity Paul is writing about is the only sort of Christianity that interests me. It is a Christianity that demands commitment, perseverance whatever the hardships, integrity whatever the temptation, contentment whatever the poverty.

Christianity like that did not come to an end with the apostle Paul. It is around now. Pierce beneath the veneer of sanctimoniousness and religiosity that you despise so much, and you will find it. An adventurous, courageous, eccentric Christianity; a Christianity that sends a brilliant mathematician to be a missionary in the South American jungle; that sends an attractive young nurse to be a Red Cross worker in Beirut; that sends a businessman earning £50,000 a year to run a hostel for down-and-outs in the East End of London. And for every story like that there are dozens of others, less dramatic in their vocation, but just as devoted in their commitment, living lives of quiet self-sacrifice for Jesus Christ.

You may not want that Christianity any more than you want any of the other kinds. It may be altogether too fanatical for your taste. But if you reject it, I suggest that it will not be because you have shown up those Christians for the hypocrites that they are, but because those Christians have shown you up for what you are: a floating voter, a spiritual 'don't know', a person who is far too scared to be committed to anything, least of all to Jesus Christ. He demands too much.

No. If there is a stumbling-block in your way, may I suggest to you that it is not really the Christians who put it there, though you may try to make out that it is. The stumbling-block is in your own lack of willingness to be *committed*. You know there are Christians whose lives you secretly admire. The question the Bible is putting to you is this: have you got the guts to be as committed to Christ as they are? Be warned: Christianity may cost you your comfort. It may cost you your health. It may cost you your bank balance. You are unlikely to get a Daimler out of it.

2. A willingness to be different (6:11-7:1)

> We have spoken freely to you, Corinthians, and opened wide our hearts to you. We are not withholding our affection from you, but you are withholding yours from us. As a fair exchange – I speak as to my children – open wide your hearts also. Do not be yoked together with unbelievers. For what do righteousness and wickedness have in common? (6:11-14)

In verse 11 Paul seems to be momentarily embarrassed by the intensity of the emotion he has been showing. He has let his tongue run away with him. His supply of rhetoric must be better than he thought for it has got the better of him for a while. 'But,' he pleads, 'can you not sense in the frankness with which I have just written, the genuine love I bear you Corinthians? There is no craftiness in what I am saying. I am not trying to manipulate you with slick words, as my rivals do when they insinuate that I don't really care about you. No, it is you who are turning the cold shoulder on me!

'How can you Corinthians believe the slanders that are circulating about me? Don't you realise that the kind of lifestyle my critics call admirable takes its cue not from Jesus, but from the unbelieving world around you? Yes,' says Paul, 'my clothes do look shabby, but then I have travelled a long way in them. Yes, my face does appear haggard, but then it has experienced a lot of stress. Yes, my body is weak with sickness, but then it has been exposed to a lot of wear and tear. Yes, my preaching does lack eloquence and sophistication, but then I am not a trained orator.' If such charges are enough to discredit Paul as an apostle – then yes, he is discredited, he agrees. 'But surely you Corinthians of all people should know that I am no charlatan. I am your spiritual father,' he says. 'It was I who brought you to Christ in the first place. How then can you be so cruel as to shut your hearts against me in this way?'

It says a great deal for Paul that he is able to speak like this to the Corinthians. After the criticism he had suffered, a proud man would have been bitter and indignant; an insecure man threatened and touchy. It says much for Paul that he only felt hurt, like a parent whose ungrateful offspring refuse to return his love. 'Be fair,' he pleads, 'I am speaking to you as my own children. Do your old man a favour, repay all of the favours he has done you.'

What is this favour that Paul desires? It is, that they stop flirting with the world as they are doing.

Do not be yoked together with unbelievers. For what do righteousness and wickedness have in common?

The picture is taken from a command, in Deuteronomy 22:10, that forbids ploughing with an ox and a donkey harnessed together. It was in fact a general principle of Moses' law, that the people of God were to avoid chequered or motley patterns, whether it was sowing two different crops together in the same field or weaving two different fibres together in the same material. It seems to have been a way of impressing on their minds the importance God places on purity. His people were not be contaminated by their pagan neighbours. They were to be holy and separate; so he educated them to have a horror of mixtures. And what Paul is doing here is explaining to us the New Testament significance of those old ceremonial laws. It is no longer a question, he says, of not yoking an ox and a donkey together; now it is a question of not yoking the church and the world together.

He gives four reasons why there can be no such liaison.

First, it is *incongruous*.

> What do righteousness and wickedness have in common? Or what fellowship can light have with darkness? What harmony is there between Christ and Belial? What does a believer have in common with an unbeliever?

A Christian and a non-Christian belong to incompatible and disjunctive realms. Good and evil, light and darkness, Christ and the devil: these are mutually exclusive categories. There is no fellowship or harmony possible between them. In a very real sense, a Christian does not belong to the same world as a non-Christian, even though he has to live in it. So it is altogether incongruous for him to try to negotiate some kind of compromise with that world.

Second it is *sacrilegious*.

> What agreement is there between the temple of God and idols? For we are the temple of the living God. As God has said: "I will live with them and walk among them, and I will be their God, and they will be my people."

Paul did not see the church as just a human club. It was a supernatural institution in which God dwelt by his Spirit, a sanctuary, the bricks of which were made up not of stone but of living people. So for the church to tangle itself up with the pagan world was not just incongruous – it was sacrilegious; it was an act of the most appalling contempt for the holy sanctuary of God.

Thirdly, it is *disobedient.*

> **Therefore come out from them and be separate, says the Lord. Touch no unclean thing, and I will receive you.**

Paul is weaving together a group of quotations from the Old Testament prophets who all spoke originally to the Jewish exiles in Babylon. They told the exiles that they were to keep themselves undefiled in their pagan environment. The same biblical commandment, says Paul, applies to the church. For we too are exiles, in a manner of speaking. We are a holy people, forced by circumstances to live in a profane culture. We are not to be corrupted by it any more than the Jewish exiles were to be. That is God's standing order for his people in every age.

Finally, it is *unprofitable.*

> **I will be a Father to you,**
> **and you will be my sons and daughters,**
> > > **says the Lord Almighty.**

There is a reward, says Paul, for the Christian who keeps himself uncompromised by the world. In the Old Testament God made a covenant pledge to the descendants of King David – 'I will be a father to him, and he will be my son' (1 Chron. 17:13). Sadly, Solomon forfeited that blessing when he foolishly brought pagan wives into his royal harem. Now we Christians are the Messianic people of the new Son of David, says Paul. We are the spiritual heirs of his promises to David. But we too will forfeit the blessing of this privileged relationship if we like Solomon compromise ourselves with unbelievers.

It all adds up to this:

> **Since we have these promises, dear friends, let us purify ourselves from everything that contaminates body and spirit, perfecting holiness out of reverence for God.**

How dare we insult the God who has so graciously adopted us into his family, by bringing shame into his household! The sanctification of God's people is no trivial matter. If you have any respect for the holiness of God, says Paul, you will realise that it is simply out of the question to be yoked together with unbelievers. If you are Christians, you must be willing to be different from the world.

That much is clear from what Paul says. But the question that perhaps arises in our minds is: What precisely does it mean in practice – being different from the world, not being yoked together with unbelievers?

It certainly does not mean that Paul is advocating monasticism. He makes that quite clear in 1 Corinthians 5:9-10, which it is important to read alongside this passage. He explains there that when he instructed Christians not to associate with sexually immoral people he did not mean non-Christians who were immoral, greedy, swindlers and idolaters; for if he had meant that, then they would have had to leave the world. No. Paul is clear that Christians must mix normally with unbelievers, otherwise how would the world be evangelised. They are not to withdraw into a holy huddle for fear of contamination.

But if he is not arguing for monasticism, what *is* Paul arguing for?

Some think the clue is to be found in the word 'yoke' in verse 14. To be yoked to somebody means that you have lost your freedom of independent movement and cannot dissociate yourself from what they are doing. Inevitably you are involved in their actions. So, some people argue, Christians are never to be so tied to unbelievers that they lose their ability to stand out as a Christian when necessary. For example, many would argue that marriage to a non-Christian constituted an unequal yoke. Some would go further and include entering a business partnership with a non-Christian, or joining a Masonic lodge or certain kinds of political parties. They argue that all these so bind a Christian that it is impossible to live a Christian life properly, if one is affiliated to them.

Others focus on the word 'fellowship' in verse 15. Literally it means 'having something in common with somebody else'. It was the word that Christians used when they spoke of the communion they experienced in the bread and wine at the Lord's Supper. So, they argue, Paul is establishing a principle here: apostate and heretical Christians must be excluded from the church's fellowship as an act of discipline. 'Separate yourselves from those who, by their lives or by their doctrine, show themselves to no longer have anything in common with true believers.'

And some have argued that these verses are forbidding Christian participation in worldly amusements such as dancing or the cinema. Indeed, over the centuries these words, 'Come out from them and be separate' have been applied by well-meaning Christian groups to almost every kind of activity that they deemed to have been compromising with the world.

What was really in Paul's mind when he penned those words? There are two observations that may help us to identify his original intention.

First, when you hear a series of rhetorical questions, such as Paul is asking in these verses, you usually expect to find that the final question is the one that most explicitly makes the speaker's point. If that is so, then the real clue to Paul's meaning would be verse 16: What agreement is there between the temple of God and idols? In that case the key word would be not 'yoke' nor 'fellowship' but 'idols'. In the absence of other evidence, I think we would have to assume that Paul is here calling the Christians in Corinth to dissociate themselves not from mixed marriages, heretical churches or dubious entertainments, but from paganism and idolatry.

Second, a great deal depends on whether you believe this paragraph is an original part of 2 Corinthians. Quite a number of scholars do not. They point out that Paul at verse 14 embarks on a digression, and that if you omit the paragraph 6:14-7:1 the text flows quite logically, from 'Open wide your hearts' to 'Make room for us in your hearts'. As the intervening section can be omitted without damaging the logic of the argument, they suggest that it must be an interpolation – perhaps a page from one of Paul's other letters to the Corinthians which we do not now possess, but which has accidentally been included.

Many books of the Bible, of course, have been put together by editors, and (as we shall see when we come to look at Chapters 10-13), 2 Corinthians may well be among them. But it has to be said that it is unlikely that this is an editorial interpolation. In all the ancient manuscripts of this letter that have come down to us, by whatever route and from whatever date, this paragraph is never missing. If it *is* an interpolation, it must have occurred at a very early stage. And it is difficult to see how a page from another letter could have been included by accident, because such evidence as we have suggests that Paul wrote his letters on continuous scrolls of papyrus. As there were no separate sheets, it would not be possible for the texts to have become mixed up.

So I believe we must proceed on the assumption that this paragraph does belong to this letter. And if that is so then we must also conclude that, while Paul's teaching doubtless has wider application to subjects such as mixed marriages and the disciplining of heresy, its original and therefore primary application must have been to these rivals who were challenging his authority at Corinth. For Paul, the version of Christianity they were offering represented compromise: compromise with pagan ideas, pagan methods, pagan vocabulary – in a word, compromise with idols. Put these two observations together and we are on safest ground if we conclude that Paul is simply begging the Corinthians here to be willing to be different, to reject the rival gospel offered by the would-be leaders in their midst: a gospel that may seem to be more 'with it', but is actually in danger of being 'without him'.

What harmony can there be between Christ and the devil? 'Make no mistake about it,' warns Paul. 'These mystery religions you are so anxious to emulate are demonic, yet you want to present the gospel as if it were just such a cult. It will not do. Christianity is different, and because it is different, you must be different too: different in the way you live, different in the way you preach. If you try to make the gospel more acceptable to the world by preaching it in a way that seems to support the world's ideas, if you market it like a mystery religion, you may make more converts. But they will not be converted to Christianity. They will be converts to this compromised, syncretised, spiritual hotch-potch of idolatry that you have invented. And I say again, it will not do.'

For Paul there can be no Christian alliance with idols. Even a sympathetic nod in the direction of paganism is out of the question. Just as it was for God's ancient people the Jews, so it is for his new covenant people the church. 'Come out from them and be separate, be different,' says the Lord. Paul is rebuking a worldliness that wants to dress Christianity up in the clothes of the world, to make it less offensive, less exclusive, less unpopular, less old-fashioned. Less different.

And that brings us right back to where we started. Why be trapped in a Datsun when you have a Daimler faith? The trouble with Prosperity Doctrine is that, like so much that passes for Christianity these days, it is just Christianity dressed up in the garb of twentieth-century secularism. No wonder the churches that preach it are so popular; which upwardly mobile member of our affluent twentieth-century Western society would not be pleased to be told, 'God loves you and has a wonderful plan for your bank balance!' But that is not Christianity; that is sanctified materialism. It is humanity doing what humanity has always done, finding religious excuses for pursuing the idols we have already made up our mind we want to pursue anyway. Humanist sociologists explain the phenomenon of religion as a 'mystification of culture'. Its function in society, they say, is comfortingly to invest secular ideas with a sacred meaning in order to reinforce the stability of the status quo. They are wrong, of course. But what an appalling indictment of the church in the West today, that there is so little evidence that can be cited to prove them wrong! Again and again we Christians show ourselves to be nothing but a rubber stamp on the world's agenda, a loud 'Amen' to the world's aspirations, an enthusiastic echo of the world's values.

Some of us are echoes of the world's left hand. Some of us – rather more of us, I suspect – are echoes of the world's right hand. But whether we practise sanctified socialism or sanctified capitalism, whether we make a virtue of our poverty or of our affluence, our Christianity has not cost us anything. It does not require any repentance of us. We are simply secular people, mouthing secular platitudes, pursuing secular goals like everyone else in our secular culture.

Real Christianity is not like that. It is willing to be different. It does not just endorse secular culture, it challenges it. As Christians, Paul tells us, we are called to a lifestyle that communicates that challenge to the world around us. We are not to be mere chameleons, indistinguishable from our cultural environment; we have got to stick out like sore thumbs. We are meant to be misfits among the world's conventions, a disturbance of the world's complacency, a question mark against the world's ideologies, a contradiction to the world's consensus, a threat to the world's psychological security. We Christians are meant to be a thorn in the world's side. 'That is how I aim to live,' says Paul. 'I will not let the world squeeze me into its mould. I am here to live as the gospel demands. If you want to be real Christians, Corinthians, that must be your aim too; you must be willing to be different.'

Tell me: what do you think the world is waiting to see before it turns to Christ? Is it really waiting to see whether we Christians can produce rock concerts as polished and professional as *Top of the Pops*? Is it really waiting to see if we can build churches as ostentatious and affluent as a City banking house? Is it really waiting to see if we can heal people's bodies as effectively as a major hospital can? Is it really waiting to see whether we Christians can be as liberal about homosexuality and as strident about feminism as any Labour-controlled borough in London can?

I suggest to you, it is not.

The world is simply waiting to see Christians who are willing to be different. The man in the street is sick and tired of bishops trying to prove how trendy their theology is. He is fed up with ecumenical conferences which try to outdo Militant Tendency in their Marxist clichés. I do not think the world is impressed in the least by the self-righteous posturing of the Moral Majority, nor by the pathetic charade of our multi-faith prayers for world peace. The world has more sense than we give it credit for. It sees all this for exactly what it is: mere secularised religion. Christians jumping on the band-wagon of contemporary enthusiasm in a pathetic attempt to woo public opinion to its side. It does not work, for the reason Jesus said it would not work. 'Salt that has lost its taste is good for nothing,' he said. And that is all that three-quarters of the 'Christianity' in this world is good for – nothing; except to be trodden contemptuously under the feet of men.

The world is looking for Christians who are willing to be totally committed to their Master, for Christians who are willing to be utterly different from itself. That is what the world is looking for; not superhuman heroics, just real Christianity, New Testament Christianity, Christianity that seeks to commend itself by its endurance, integrity and its refusal to conform.

Why, in God's name, is that kind of committed, distinctive and contented Christianity so hard to find? Could it be, perhaps, that we are all too busy praying for Daimlers?

8

Two Kinds of Repentance
(2 Corinthians 7:2-16)

Make room for us in your hearts. We have wronged no one, we have corrupted no one, we have exploited no one. I do not say this to condemn you; I have said before that you have such a place in our hearts that we would live or die with you. I have great confidence in you; I take great pride in you. I am greatly encouraged; in all our troubles my joy knows no bounds.

For when we came into Macedonia, this body of ours had no rest, but we were harassed at every turn – conflicts on the outside, fears within. But God, who comforts the downcast, comforted us by the coming of Titus, and not only by his coming but also by the comfort you had given him. He told us about your longing for me, your deep sorrow, your ardent concern for me, so that my joy was greater than ever.

Even if I caused you sorrow by my letter, I do not regret it. Though I did regret it – I see that my letter hurt you, but only for a little while – yet now I am happy, not because you were made sorry, but because your sorrow led you to repentance. For you became sorrowful as God intended and so were not harmed in any way by us. Godly sorrow brings repentance that leads to salvation and leaves no regret, but worldly sorrow brings death. See what this godly sorrow has produced in you: what earnestness, what eagerness to clear yourselves, what indignation, what alarm, what longing, what concern, what readiness to see justice done. At every point you have proved yourselves to be innocent in this matter. So even though I wrote to you, it was not on account of the one who did the wrong or of the injured party, but rather that before God you could see for yourselves how devoted to us you are. By all this we are encouraged.

In addition to our own encouragement, we were especially delighted to see how happy Titus was, because his spirit has been refreshed by all of you. I had boasted to him about you, and you have not embarrassed me. But just as everything we said to you was true, so our boasting about you to Titus has proved to be true as well. And his affection for you is all the greater when he remembers that you were all obedient, receiving him with fear and trembling. I am glad I can have complete confidence in you (2 Corinthians 7:2-16).

WHEN WAS THE LAST TIME YOU CRIED? I find children's films the worst tear-jerkers. It's been like that with me ever since Bambi! My only comfort is that I am not quite such a sucker for sentiment as the mother who confessed to me some time ago that both she and her four year-old had been reduced to blubbering heaps by the Care Bears movie!

On a more serious note, there are, of course, less artificial reasons for weeping. Physical pain is one of them. People in good health do not realise how emotionally gruelling chronic illness can be. Or perhaps you have experienced a deep, personal bereavement; there are few places where tears are more common than at a graveside.

In this chapter, however, I want to talk about a different kind of sorrow, and one which is little understood today, though it is far from rare. I want to talk about sorrow for sin, about tears of repentance. Have you ever shed any of those? The Corinthians had; indeed, it could be said that is the one thing they had in their favour. Paul talks again and again, in this passage, about how they were 'made sorry'.

The first three verses (7:2-4) represent the completion of Paul's long self defence that has occupied the previous chapters. 'Make room for us in your hearts,' Paul says in summary. 'We have wronged no-one, we have corrupted no-one, we have exploited no-one.' The charges being made about him are all false.

His relationship with the Corinthian church was strained, however, for another reason in addition to the hostility of his rivals. It is one that you might easily have forgotten, for though Paul did introduce it in the opening chapters, he went off at a tangent at 2:14 and has not really mentioned the matter since. But here at last in Chapter 7 he is returning to finish off what he began there. To set the scene, you may want to turn back to Chapter 2, 'Love Hurts'. There, you will remember, we discovered that Paul had been involved in a disciplinary problem: the need to issue a public rebuke to a church member who had committed a grave, though unspecified, offence.

Three things emerged from that earlier discussion of the matter: first, the Corinthian church had initially ignored the matter; second, Paul was not prepared to accept this failure to discipline; and third, the matter, so far as Paul was concerned, warranted both a sharp letter of rebuke to the church and also a visit from Titus to ensure that the letter had been heeded and acted upon.

It is against this background that our passage is set, and if you bear Chapter 2 in mind you will be able to understand it more easily. In 2:12-13, Paul tells us that he has been so distressed about the disciplinary crisis in Corinth that he could not settle down to his missionary work in Asia, even though he had an outstanding preaching opportunity in Troas. He was strangely restless, and his anxiety was further exacerbated when Titus was late returning from the diplomatic mission to Corinth on which Paul had sent him. In fact so disturbed did Paul become that he actually abandoned his work in Asia and took a ship across the Aegean Sea to Macedonia, in the hope of meeting Titus at the earliest possible moment. Judging from 7:5, however, you will see that even this did not quell his apprehension. 'When we came into Macedonia, this body of ours had no rest, but we were harassed at every turn – conflicts on the outside, fears within.'

It seems that he was concerned that the anti-Pauline faction which he knew was active at Corinth might have so irreparably soured the atmosphere that his reputation had been destroyed there. And that would mean two things. It would mean a very cool and uncooperative welcome for his young colleague Titus which would not only be uncomfortable for him but dangerous as well. For Paul knew that Corinth was a hostile place for a lonely preacher. He had spent eighteen months there and he had been afraid for his life most of the time. If Titus could not rely on the protection of the Christian community in the city, he might very easily get himself into big trouble.

But it seems clear that Paul was also worried about the letter he had sent. It was so sharp! Would it damage his own reputation in the church at Corinth even further? In a way he had played into his rivals' hands by sending such a letter. It was not difficult to imagine how they might exploit it. 'Oh, that Paul – he is just a peevish, narrow-minded old belly-acher! That's all he is!' The letter would fuel their conspiracy to discredit him. So had he been wrong to send it? Would it have been politically wiser to adopt a more conciliatory tone, instead of reprimanding the believers at Corinth in such an uncompromising manner? In verse 12 one can detect that Paul was aware he was taking a calculated risk. The reaction of the Corinthians to his letter would be a clear indication of just how far Paul's authority had been eroded in the church there.

On top of all the stress generated by these two matters – his concern for Titus' safety, and the general situation in Corinth and the possibly increasing antipathy towards him – when Paul got to Macedonia it seems he was put under even more pressure by some kind of additional, external harassment, 'Conflicts on the outside.' Maybe Paul is referring to opposition from the Macedonian authorities, who may well have remembered this Paul as the Jew who a few years earlier had caused a public riot in Philippi, demolished the city jail in an earthquake, and humiliated the civil authorities by demanding a public apology for wrongful imprisonment. It would not be in the least surprising if the immigration officers in Macedonia were keen to get this known troublemaker out of the province as soon as possible, and were applying some pressure to achieve it.

So how encouraging it must have been when at long last Titus turned up, safe and well; and, moreover, with the good news that the crisis at Corinth seemed at last to be resolving itself.

> **God, who comforts the downcast, comforted us by the coming of Titus, and not only by his coming but also by the comfort you had given him. He told us about your longing for me, your deep sorrow, your ardent concern for me, so that my joy was greater than ever** (7:6-7).

There is an overwhelming sense of relief that breathes through those verses. Of course, the rival party was still active in Corinth, but the vast majority of the believers in the church were loyal to Paul; that was the good news Titus had brought. They entertained the fondest memories of him, and as a result all Paul's fears about Titus not being well-received had proved groundless. On the contrary, they had welcomed the young man with open arms. 'Well,' says Paul in the last paragraph of the chapter (with the confidence, I suspect, of relaxed and unburdened hindsight), 'I knew you would really. I knew you would not let me down. I told Titus before he left: Don't worry about the Corinthians, they are a warm-hearted bunch, they will look after you.'

But how pleased Paul was (and privately relieved) that his assurances had not proved over-optimistic! 'In addition to our own encouragement, we were especially delighted to see how happy Titus was, because his spirit has been refreshed by all of you. I had boasted to him about you ... and ... our boasting about you to Titus has proved to be true as well' (verses 13-14). Titus had been treated with such respect and honour that he had been deeply touched by the experience of meeting them all. 'His affection for you is all the greater when he remembers that you were all obedient, receiving him with fear and trembling' (verse 15).

'You Corinthians!' he says. 'You have really come through the test with flying colours just as I hoped you would. I am so glad I can have complete confidence in you.'

But it was the way that the Corinthians had received Paul's letter, even more than the way that they had received Titus, that particularly gratified and relieved the apostle. He knew that what he had written was bound to make the Corinthians feel bad, because he had really spelt out that by failing to discipline the offender they were accomplices in his sin and were ignoring Paul's apostolic authority.

But the question in Paul's mind was this: what kind of sadness would the Corinthians feel? For he knew that when it comes to sin and failure there are two kinds of sorrow. And Paul's discussion of those two kinds of sorrow in 7:8-13 gives this chapter its special value for us today. It introduces that subject of tears with which we began. The key verse is verse 10:

> **Godly sorrow brings repentance that leads to salvation and leaves no regret, but worldly sorrow brings death.**

I want to try to clarify for you the contrast Paul is making here between godly sorrow and worldly sorrow, because I believe it is an immensely important one. Feelings of guilt and failure cause people many more tears than you can imagine, but what kind of tears are they? What kind of repentance do they evidence? That is the question. It is vital to realise that not all sorrow for sin is a godly sorrow. Not all tears of self-reproach that people shed lead them to salvation. On the contrary, Paul says, some such tears are lethal, they lead to death.

If you are going to eat mushrooms, you had better learn what a toadstool looks like. In the same way, if you are going to feel sorry for your sins, you had better learn the difference between godly sorrow and worldly sorrow. Let me help you distinguish between them.

1. Godly sorrow is always appropriate to the circumstances
Why does Paul not regret causing the Corinthians sorrow?

> **For you became sorrowful as God intended and so were not harmed in any way by us** (7:9).

It is important to realise that there are some kinds of sorrow of which Paul could not have said that; some do cause damage to people. Consider these words of Tony Lewis, writing in *The Guardian* some years ago:

> Until I became ill, I had neither experienced depression nor observed it in others. I knew of a few people who had had mental breakdowns, but the term meant nothing to me. If anything I looked down on them as being weak, spineless people whom society would do well to be rid of. And when a psychiatrist told me I was mentally ill, I was horrified. [1]

---

1. Down But Not Out by Tony Lewis. *The Guardian*, 5th May, 1982

He goes on in his article to speak of how ashamed he felt, as the advance of his depressive condition rendered him more and more helpless and guilt-ridden. It grew from something mild and infrequent into what he calls 'a brutal scourge, which I believed I could escape only through death'.

Paul could never pretend that sorrow of that kind is innocuous, or that it leaves no regret. Plainly it is not so. Psychiatric depression is a vicious curse that quite definitely belongs in the category of 'worldly sorrow'; for in a considerable number of cases it quite literally brings death. As many as one in ten seriously depressed people attempt suicide. Unfortunately, some of them succeed. So what is the difference between this self-destructive melancholy and the godly sorrow that Paul wants to commend to us in this paragraph?

The difference is simple but enormously important. The sorrow for sin which is characteristic of abnormal and unhealthy minds is always inappropriate sorrow.

Sometimes it is inappropriate because the sin over which it grieves is *totally imaginary*. The depressed person may be reduced to abject despair about appalling crimes which they have never committed, although they sincerely believe they have.

Sometimes the sadness is inappropriate because it is *grossly exaggerated*. The depressed person may feel intensely about some failure in a way that is out of all proportion to its real seriousness. A speck of dust on the carpet will generate as much anxiety in the person as if they were personally responsible for dropping the Hiroshima bomb. A minor scrape in the car precipitates as shattering a sense of guilt and failure as if they had been convicted for murder.

Either way, the sorrow is inappropriate. It reflects guilt which is either the product of delusion or irrationality.

But this was not the case at Corinth. Paul had written his letter because a real sin had been committed and the church's failure to discipline it represented a serious act of negligence. The sorrow that the letter caused was quite appropriate to the circumstances. That was why Paul did not regret his part in generating it. This is a most important observation. One of the most disturbing effects of humanistic psychiatry in our century has been the general weakening of people's understanding of 'appropriate guilt'. We are assured by learned men that morality is just a matter of social convention; that our sense of right and wrong is merely a result of behavioural conditioning received as children; that our conscience is just our infantile experience of parental authority internalised as a Freudian super-ego, and so on. And the implication frequently is that guilt-feelings should therefore not be taken seriously and are indeed better ignored, because to be preoccupied with them is unwholesome. For many in our generation *all* guilt is regarded as inappropriate and unhealthy. We no longer speak of 'conviction of sin' and send the guilt-stricken person to a pastor for counselling. We speak of a 'guilt-complex' and send the guilt-stricken person to a psychiatrist for therapy.

The consequences can be morally dangerous, as Anna Russell's *Psychiatric Folk Song* testifies:

> I went to my psychiatrist to be psychoanalysed
> To find out why I killed the cat and blacked my husband's eye.
> He laid me on a downy couch to see what he could find,
> And here's what he dredged up, from my subconscious mind.
> When I was one, my mummy hid my dolly in a trunk
> And so it follows, naturally, that I am always drunk.
> When I was two, I saw my father kiss the maid one day,
> And that is why I suffer from kleptomania.
> At three I had a feeling of ambivalence towards my brothers
> And so it follows naturally I poisoned all my lovers.
> But I am happy now I have learned the lesson this has taught:
> Everything I do that's wrong, is someone else's fault!

Sadly, many people are drawing similar conclusions. This guilt-denying attitude is very prevalent today. I have to say that, though I have enormous sympathy for people who suffer guilt feelings unnecessarily – feelings often coloured by mental illness or by neurotic traits in their personalities – nevertheless real guilt exists. It is perfectly normal and healthy. We cannot escape that guilt by reclassifying it as psychiatric illness. It is an objective condition of our hearts and lives as sinners before a righteous God. It is not just a subjective state of mind.

So the goal of a Christian counsellor is not to eliminate all guilt-feelings from people. To attempt to do so is wrong, and Paul did not try. The task of the Christian counsellor is to ensure that the guilt people feel is appropriate to their circumstances. Christianity is not a happiness pill; there are times when people ought to feel sad. In Paul's judgment, this was such an occasion in the experience of the Corinthians. That is why he could say, 'You have become sorrowful as God intended, and I do not regret it, even if I caused you sorrow, because you have not been harmed by it.' Godly sorrow is appropriate sorrow – sorrow generated by real sins not imaginary ones, guilt that is proportional to the real seriousness of those sins, not irrationally exaggerated.

When you and I feel guilty, then the first question we must ask ourselves is: 'What am I guilty about? What have I done? How serious is it?' Always be suspicious of vague feelings of unworthiness. The Holy Spirit is never vague! If he wants to convict us of a sin it will be a specific sin – identifiable acts, identifiable words, identifiable thoughts. It will be a sin you can put a name to and probably a date. Vague and ill-defined feelings of failure are much more likely to be the devil's territory than the Holy Spirit's. For the devil has an interest in keeping us demoralised, paralysed by our sense of defeat. And I assure you there is no weapon more effective in his hands for that purpose than a really well-developed inferiority complex. The devil loves perfectionists! He loves them because perfectionists always set themselves hopelessly elevated expectations. It does not matter how well they do, they always feel themselves failures at the end of it. Little wonder that they have no self-esteem and are always apologising to everybody.

Guilt, for people like that, is a way of life: it is a knee-jerk reaction to just about everything that happens around them, whether they are responsible for it or not. They assume that any little imperfection they detect is their own fault. If you pay them a compliment they never accept it. 'He does not really know me,' they say to themselves. 'If he really knew me, he would despise me. Probably he *does* despise me really and is just pretending ...' And you dare not offer them even the most tactfully-worded criticism, because if they can interpret your words as a slap in the face you can be sure that they will. 'You have to be careful with old so-and-so,' it's said of them. 'He is a very sensitive person.' But old so-and-so's problem is not sensitivity. It is irrational guilt, it is worldly sorrow that he suffers from.

God intends us to experience only appropriate, godly sorrow. It is not tied to vague feelings. It is always a response to real sins. So if you are feeling guilty today, the first thing you must do is ask God to show you why. Identify the specific thing that the Holy Spirit is convicting you about. And if there is nothing specific you can put your finger on, I suggest that you shake your shoulders very hard, because it is very likely that the devil is sitting on one of them!

2. Godly sorrow is always practical in its expression

> See what this godly sorrow has produced in you: what earnestness, what eagerness to clear yourselves, what indignation, what alarm, what longing, what concern, what readiness to see justice done. At every point you have proved yourselves to be innocent in this matter (7:11).

If there is sorrow for sin that is inappropriate and irrational, it must also be said that there is a sorrow for sin that is insincere and superficial. In the Old Testament Moses repeatedly came to Pharaoh, demanding in the name of God that he release the Israelite slaves or face the consequences. And again and again, Pharaoh said, 'No.' Each time he refused, God sent a plague on the land. At first they were fairly tame: pollution in the River Nile, frogs in the city, swarms of gnats and flies over the land – but as time wore on and

Pharaoh became increasingly obstinate, so the plagues became increasingly grave. Animals began to die, people began to suffer, hailstorms devastated the crops. As the plagues became more threatening, Pharaoh repented – or at least, he claimed to do so. 'The Lord is right,' he said, 'I am wrong. Pray that the Lord will take this thunder and hail away, we have had enough of it, and I will let you go.' But no sooner had Moses asked God to stop the plague than Pharaoh's old resistance re-emerged. He repented of his repentance. And when the next plague descended, the same pattern was repeated. 'Forgive my sins,' said Pharaoh – but when the plague disappeared, so did his concern for pardon.

That kind of superficial and insincere sorrow for sin is far from uncommon. There are many varieties of it. Sometimes, as in Pharaoh's case, it is what one might call 'crisis repentance'. People only pretend to feel sorry for their sins, in an attempt to get God on their side in an emergency. You can probably think of people, as I can, who seemed to discover immense concern for spiritual things when illness struck their family, but now the crisis is over, they are nowhere to be seen.

Sometimes it is what you might call 'ritual repentance', just like the Pharisees in Jesus' day. There are some people who make a great song-and-dance about going to the priest to make their confession. They are very pleased to be asked to perform all kinds of penance, provided it is of a purely ritual nature like saying prayers or lighting a candle. But they will come back next week, confessing exactly the same sins. Nothing ever changes in their lives; repentance is for them just a habit, a routine like going to the laundry or the post office. And it is performed just as thoughtlessly and superficially.

But perhaps the most insidious of all forms of insincere sorrow for sin is 'manipulative repentance': the kind of self-reproach which is designed to extract sympathy from other people. We have all observed the crocodile tears of the sulky child who thinks that a suitable display of misery will turn an angry parent into an indulgent one. There are many adults who produce exactly the same kind of artificial sorrow. They learn, either consciously or subconsciously, that looking depressed can gain attention for them from others who would otherwise ignore them. In this modern world there is even a certain status in being 'depressed'. You can almost boast of it; and if you do, vast numbers of doctors and counsellors – and of course Christians – take an enormous interest in you. No wonder that some people never seem to change for the better; there are too many advantages in appearing pathetic and morose. Indeed, there are some, like Mrs Gummidge in Charles Dickens' *David Copperfield*, who enjoy feeling miserable. Sorrow is for them a kind of masochistic self-indulgence, rather like flagellation may have been for some medieval monks.

We must never think that because somebody looks sorry, feels sorry or even says 'sorry' for their sins that this must necessarily be a case of godly sorrow.

There are all kinds of worldly sorrow that may seem convincing on the surface but are in fact mere counterfeits. How can we tell the difference?

It is quite simple. Godly sorrow always issues in practical actions, designed to put things right. Take the Corinthians, for instance. Paul knew there was nothing superficial or insincere about their sorrow. He knew it was real, godly sorrow. Why? Because of the way they responded to it. 'See what this godly sorrow has produced in you,' he says (verse 11). And he goes on to list what he meant.

'Earnestness', to begin with. The word has an energy to it. These people did not just sit, helplessly shrugging their shoulders, whimpering 'Oh, what a mess I am in!' They were going to do something about it. Godly sorrow always produces such energy. He speaks of 'eagerness to clear yourselves'. They wanted to make up for their failure in any way they could. He speaks about 'indignation', which means not indignation against Paul for accusing them but against the offender whose sin had been such an embarrassment to them. He speaks about 'alarm' (literally, fear), because the moral seriousness of their situation had become plain to them, and the possibility of

God's judgment was all too real. And he speaks about 'readiness to see justice done'. Literally the word means 'vengeance' or 'retribution', and it is a reference to the fact that, as we read in 2:6, the offender in question had been punished by the church: almost certainly by some form of public rebuke. Because that disciplinary action had now been taken, Paul could say, 'At every point you have proved yourselves innocent in this matter' – not innocent of negligence, of course, because plainly they had been very slow to engage in this act of pastoral discipline; but they were now innocent of complicity in the offender's crime, because as a congregation they had publicly dissociated themselves from it as Paul had insisted they should. The seriousness of the man's sin had been acknowledged and its reproach had been lifted from the church as a whole, because they had seen justice done in the matter.

This is precisely the kind of active and practical response that can be expected when repentance is real. Think of Zacchaeus the tax collector, whom we read about in Luke's Gospel. He was a man who had spent his life feathering his nest by exploiting his fellow-countrymen. When he became a Christian, what do we find him saying? 'I give half of my possessions to the poor, and if I have cheated anybody out of anything, I will pay back four times the amount' (Luke 19:8). There must have been quite a queue outside Zacchaeus' front door that day! But so it ought to be. Godly sorrow always expresses itself in such practical ways.

Again, there is a very important lesson for us here. If you are feeling guilty about sin, do not be content merely to wallow in mournful feelings about your failure. Repentance is not simply an emotional response, but a practical one. Get up, make plans to do something about it. There may be restitution you need to make, as Zacchaeus did. There may be new habits you need to cultivate; there may be apologies you need to offer. God is not interested in sorrow that simply makes an exhibition of itself in order to win sympathy or attention of others. Godly sorrow is always practical in its expression.

As John the Baptist put it, real repentance always brings forth fruit in people's lives. Therein, I believe, lies one of the dangers of mass evangelism. Sometimes it seems to be content simply to obtain a mental decision. But real repentance does not end with decisions, it ends in actions.

Real repentance has practical, observable, behavioural consequences in people. So you had an emotional experience at an evangelistic meeting? So you signed your name on a card? So you held your hand up for the evangelist to see? These can be very valid symbols of an inner change, but real repentance is not just about feeling affected, it is about doing righteousness. So if a businessman turns to Christ and is repentant, sharp practice has to stop; the money he has defrauded from his customers has to be returned. That is repentance. If a housewife is converted, repentance means that the backbiting and malicious gossip has to stop. She has to go to her neighbour and say that she is sorry for the wrong things she has said. If a sophisticated member of our permissive society becomes a Christian, repentance means that the sleeping around has to stop; new habits of chastity have to be cultivated.

This is what it is all about. Beware of superficial repentance. The road to hell is paved with good intentions. But real repentance requires action. It does something practical about the sin which the Holy Spirit has exposed.

3. Godly sorrow is always God-centred in its direction

'Godly sorrow' is literally, in Paul's original, 'according-to-God sorrow'. It is sorrow, in other words, that has God as its focus. For the thing about worldly sorrow which is perhaps more characteristic of it than anything else is that it is always self-centred. That is how you recognise it. Ask a person suffering from worldly sorrow why they are unhappy, and in nine cases out of ten they do not tell you, 'Because I have sinned against God'; they tell you, 'Because I feel fed up with myself.' Worldly sorrow, in fact, is just another name for self-pity. I have let myself down, I have failed to achieve my goals. It may look like humility, but in fact it is humiliation. And humiliation is often just another word for wounded pride.

Such people do not feel sorry for their sins at all, they feel sorry for themselves. And it is because of the fundamentally self-directed orientation of their sorrow that worldly sorrow has such a damning consequence in them. Paul says, 'Worldly sorrow brings death.' It certainly does. Judas is a classic example. He committed the ultimate treachery, betraying Christ for thirty pieces of silver. But Matthew tells us that in the aftermath of that crime he became overwhelmed with remorse: '"I have sinned, for I have betrayed innocent blood"... then he went away and hanged himself' (Matt. 27:4-5).

There are those who say that this proves that Judas repented. I wish it did, but I am afraid that suicide is never an act of penitence. Suicide is the ultimate act of self-pity and self-despair. Judas' sorrow, like all worldly sorrow, was self-centred; and self-centred sorrow is always going to end up as hopeless sorrow. For the one person you can never forgive is yourself. No matter how hard the psychotherapist bolsters your self-esteem, no matter how hard he works to boost your self-image, no matter how hard he encourages your self-confidence – if the guilt on your conscience is real guilt, as opposed to some neurotic exaggeration or insane delusion, then the more in touch with reality his therapy brings you, the more, not less, guilty you are going to feel.

Perhaps you recall Macbeth's famous enquiry of the doctor regarding his wife's conscience-stricken behaviour, in Shakespeare's play.

> Canst thou not minister to a mind diseased,
> Pluck from the memory a rooted sorrow,
> Raze out the written troubles of the brain,
> And with some sweet oblivious antidote
> Cleanse the stuff'd bosom of that perilous stuff
> Which weighs upon the heart?

Do you remember the physician's reply?

> ... Therein the patient
> Must minister to himself.

That is the reply that twentieth-century psychiatry ultimately gives too. 'Therein the patient must minister to himself.' Worldly sorrow is focused around self, and so it is from self-therapy of one kind or another that it must seek its remedy. But I suggest to you that it finds none; not where real guilt is concerned. There is no 'sweet oblivious antidote' to real guilt. The sentence we need to hear, when like Lady Macbeth we pace the floor, rendered sleepless with pangs of conscience because real guilt lies on our hands, is the one sentence we can never say to ourselves: 'Your sins are forgiven you.'

Only God can say that. Only God can forgive sins, and that is why only godly sorrow can ever issue in hope. For godly sorrow has God, not self, as its focus. And that is why Paul can say that it leads to salvation.

If Judas is the classic example of the death that worldly sorrow brings in its wake, then the classic example of the salvation that godly sorrow brings in its wake is surely Peter. One of the twelve disciples like Judas, he failed dreadfully that first Good Friday just as Judas did. He denied the Master not just once, but three times. If Peter's life had still been centred around himself, I have little doubt that remorse would have driven him that night to the same tragic extremity that it drove Judas. But Peter did not commit suicide. He dared to believe that he, failure as he was, still had hope.

It was not hope born of his own strength. He knew that night that he had none. It was hope born of God's grace; and in finding the way out of his pit of despair that night, Peter was discovering what every Christian must discover: that it is only when the self-centredness of our worldly sorrow gives way to the God-centredness of godly sorrow, that our experience of guilt ceases to be a dead end and becomes instead a doorway to salvation. As Peter himself wrote, 'He himself bore our sins in his body on the tree, so that we might die to sins and live for righteousness; by his wounds you have been healed' (1 Pet. 2:24).

Perhaps as you are reading this chapter you are saying to yourself, 'This teaching is all very well for those who need it. But I am all right.' You do not feel guilty; perhaps you have never felt guilty. Perhaps tears of repentance are something you could hardly imagine yourself shedding.

If that is your situation, you may not feel sorry for yourself, but I assure you I feel most dreadfully sorry for you. For there is such a thing as real guilt, and one day you will find that out. Sooner or later the real guilt that lies on your heart, as it lies on mine and everybody else's, will become plain to you. If you knew your real condition, you would not feel gratified that you know nothing of godly sorrow. Godly sorrow is a blessing.

But some of you who are reading this do feel guilt-stricken. A sense of failure dogs your heels. There are many, many people like you; people who suffer in their own private hell of remorse and self-reproach. I want to say to you, first of all: Why do you feel guilty? Is it real guilt? Can you name the sins? Can you tell me when you performed them? Or is it just vague feelings of unworthiness? Dismiss the latter; concentrate on the former.

Second, what can you do practically to express your repentance of those sins? What restitution can you make? What new habits can you cultivate? What apologies can you offer? Take practical action to show that your repentance is not wallowing in self-pity but a real concern to put matters right in your life. Do it!

Third, look up to God in your situation. Stop putting yourself at the centre of the stage. That is why there is so much self-pity in what you feel. Put something bigger there, something bigger even than your sin. There is something bigger, you know: the cross where Jesus died. The grace of God which became available to us, through his death, is bigger even than those sins that lie on your conscience. Focus your mind on that and your sorrow will not be worldly sorrow; it will be 'according to God' sorrow. And it will lead you to salvation.

This is the secret psychiatrists all over the world are searching for. They know how many people there are who need to pass from self-rejection and self-torture into a new self-respect founded on a clear conscience. Unfortunately human psychiatry cannot offer it – not to people who are really guilty. But God can; that is what the gospel is all about.

9

Christian Giving
(2 Corinthians 8:1-9:15)

And now, brothers, we want you to know about the grace that God has given the Macedonian churches. Out of the most severe trial, their over-flowing joy and their extreme poverty welled up in rich generosity. For I testify that they gave as much as they were able, and even beyond their ability. Entirely on their own, they urgently pleaded with us for the privilege of sharing in this service to the saints. And they did not do as we expected, but they gave themselves first to the Lord and then to us in keeping with God's will. So we urged Titus, since he had earlier made a beginning, to bring also to completion this act of grace on your part. But just as you excel in everything – in faith, in speech, in knowledge, in complete earnestness and in your love for us – see that you also excel in this grace of giving.

I am not commanding you, but I want to test the sincerity of your love by comparing it with the earnestness of others. For you know the grace of our Lord Jesus Christ, that though he was rich, yet for your sakes he became poor, so that you through his poverty might become rich.

And here is my advice about what is best for you in this matter: Last year you were the first not only to give but also to have the desire to do so. Now finish the work, so that your eager willingness to do it may be matched by your completion of it, according to your means. For if the willingness is there, the gift is acceptable according to what one has, not according to what he does not have.

Our desire is not that others might be relieved while you are hard pressed, but that there might be equality. At the present time your plenty will supply what they need, so that in turn their plenty will supply what you need. Then there will be equality, as it is written: "He who gathered much did not have too much, and he who gathered little did not have too little."

I thank God, who put into the heart of Titus the same concern I have for you. For Titus not only welcomed our appeal, but he is coming to you with much enthusiasm and on his own initiative. And we are sending along with him the brother who is praised by all the churches for his service to the gospel. What is more, he was chosen by the churches to accompany us as we carry the offering, which we administer in order to honour the Lord himself and to show our eagerness to help. We want to avoid any criticism of the way we administer this liberal gift. For we are taking pains to do what is right, not only in the eyes of the Lord but also in the eyes of men.

In addition, we are sending with them our brother who has often proved to us in many ways that he is zealous, and now even more so because of his great confidence in you. As for Titus, he is my partner and fellow worker among you; as for our brothers, they are representatives of the churches and an honour to Christ. Therefore show these men the proof of your love and the reason for our pride in you, so that the churches can see it.

There is no need for me to write to you about this service to the saints. For I know your eagerness to help, and I have been boasting about it to the Macedonians, telling them that since last year you in Achaia were ready to give; and your enthusiasm has stirred most of them to action. But I am sending the brothers in order that our boasting about you in this matter should not prove hollow, but that you may be ready, as I said you would be. For if any Macedonians come with me and find you unprepared, we – not to say anything about you – would be ashamed of having been so confident. So I thought it necessary to urge the brothers to visit you in advance and finish the arrangements for the generous gift you had promised. Then it will be ready as a generous gift, not as one grudgingly given.

Remember this: Whoever sows sparingly will also reap sparingly, and whoever sows generously will also reap generously. Each man should give what he has decided in his heart to give, not reluctantly or under compulsion, for God loves a cheerful giver. And God is able to make all grace abound to you, so that in all things at all times, having all that you need, you will abound in every good work. As it is written:

> "He has scattered abroad his gifts to the poor;
> his righteousness endures forever."

Now he who supplies seed to the sower and bread for food will also supply and increase your store of seed and will enlarge the harvest of your righteousness. You will be made rich in every way so that you can be generous on every occasion, and through us your generosity will result in thanksgiving to God.

This service that you perform is not only supplying the needs of God's people but is also overflowing in many expressions of thanks to God. Because of the service by which you have proved yourselves, men will praise God for the obedience that accompanies your confession of the gospel of Christ, and for your generosity in sharing with them and with everyone else. And in their prayers for you their hearts will go out to you, because of the surpassing grace God has given you. Thanks be to God for his indescribable gift! (2 Corinthians 8:1-9:15).

THESE CHAPTERS REVEAL WHY IT WAS SO IMPORTANT THAT PAUL SHOULD FEEL CONFIDENT IN THE CORINTHIANS. In addition to all his missionary activity in Asia and Europe, he was organising a charitable fund and he was expecting the Corinthians to contribute to it. He does not make clear what the fund was, but I am sure it is the same one that he mentions elsewhere in the New Testament; notably in the letter to the Romans: 'I am on my way to Jerusalem in the service of the saints there. For [the churches in] Macedonia and Achaia were pleased to make a contribution for the poor among the saints in Jerusalem' (Romans 15:25-26).

The church in Jerusalem had been the victim of poverty right from its beginning, no doubt partly as a result of the hostility of the Jewish populace there and partly because of a famine that we read about in the book of Acts. Paul seems to have felt a special obligation to relieve this need. He tells us in his letter to the Galatians that the last time he was in Jerusalem he promised Peter that he would do everything he could to help the poor Christians there with funds from the Gentile churches. The most obvious source of such benevolent funds were the churches of Greece, and particularly the wealthy urban centres in Achaia: churches like Corinth. And to give them their due, judging from 8:10 the early signs were that the Christians there responded very well to Paul's charitable appeal for this fund. He says that Corinth was not only the first church to make a contribution; it also pledged further money in future.

Indeed, in 1 Corinthians 16, we find Paul giving instructions about how they were to take a collection for the relief fund every Sunday, and to gather together the monies thus obtained so that a good-sized lump would be on deposit and available the moment he arrived, so that he could take it on to Jerusalem. Unfortunately it seems that in the twelve months since the launch of the fund the Corinthians' initial enthusiasm had waned. Perhaps it was the undermining influence of that anti-Paul rival faction of which we have spoken so much that caused it. Anyway reading between the lines, it is clear that Paul felt some anxiety lest the much-publicised pledge that the Corinthians had made to this fund was not going to materialise.

> I know your eagerness to help, and I have been boasting
> about it to the Macedonians, telling them that since last year
> you in Achaia were ready to give; and your enthusiasm has
> stirred most of them to action. But I am sending the brothers
> in order that our boasting about you in this matter should
> not prove hollow, but that you may be ready, as I said you
> would be (9:2-3).

It seems that Paul did not want either himself or the Corinthians
to be embarrassed by discovering that the money they had promised
was not ready on time. So having been reassured by Titus that the
Corinthians still entertained great affection and support for him, he
includes these two chapters in his letter, urging the Christians there
to renew their commitment to his famine-relief fund. 'You have had
over a year now,' he says, 'and I am anxious to finalise the account
and get the money where it is needed.' Indeed, you could say that in
these chapters Paul is really writing for us a model Christian
begging letter. He is telling us why, as Christians, we should give.

1. Giving is a mark of Christian discipleship (8:1-7)

> Brothers, we want you to know about the grace that God has
> given the Macedonian churches (8:1)

Every teacher knows that nothing gets the best out of a group of
children like a little good-natured competition with another class or
school. In a sense Paul is fostering just such gentle rivalry here. He
was in Macedonia, the northern province of Greece, while he was
writing this letter. Apparently the response of the Macedonians to
his appeal had been impressive. Places like Philippi and Thessalonica had really gone out of their way to give. What better goad with
which to encourage the Corinthians, than a little loud praise for their
country cousins up north! The implication is: you do not want to be
outdone by them, do you?

Some of us may feel it was rather disreputable of the apostle to
use this kind of tactic. Does it not border on emotional blackmail

when he continues: 'I want to test the sincerity of your love by comparing it with the earnestness of others' (8:8). But in Paul's defence it has to be said that the Macedonian churches he is using to challenge the Corinthians' generosity could scarcely have been perceived as a serious threat to Corinthian prestige. They were much smaller, much less affluent congregations. Frankly, if wealthy Corinth could not raise more funds than Philippi and Thessalonica, then they fully deserved to be humiliated. Just as indeed we deserve to be embarrassed when we hear of the extraordinary generosity of some Third World churches in Africa, India, or Latin America compared with the meagre tithes that we so often offer from our affluence. No: it can hardly be called emotional blackmail when it is the gifts of the poor that are providing moral leverage on the parsimoniousness of the rich.

But there is no denying that, in the Macedonians' case, the moral leverage was quite irresistible. See what he says about them.

(a) The sacrificial nature of their giving

> **Out of the most severe trial, their overflowing joy and their extreme poverty welled up in rich generosity. For I testify that they gave as much as they were able, and even beyond their ability** (8:2-3a).

Macedonia had an exploited, colonial economy, and on top of that the Christians there had to suffer a great deal of persecution. Many of the believers had been fined or dispossessed of their property. So much so, that Paul can say that their poverty was 'extreme' – it had hit rock-bottom. And yet instead of using their lack of resources as an excuse for reducing their contribution, the Macedonian experience of want had had the strange effect of multiplying their liberality. They gave far beyond what could be reasonably expected from them in their situation. It was, says Paul, extraordinarily sacrificial generosity.

(b) The gratifying enthusiasm of their giving

Entirely on their own, they urgently pleaded with us for the privilege of sharing in this service to the saints (8:3b,4).

Paul did not have to twist their arms to get them to contribute. They spontaneously volunteered to give. In fact this is the basis of Paul's irony in verse 4: 'they begged,' he says, but not for money to relieve their own poverty. No, they were 'begging' for the opportunity to help to relieve the poverty of others. They counted such an opportunity a privilege, literally 'a grace'. They really believed what the Lord Jesus said: that it is more blessed to give than to receive. As far as they were concerned, they were the lucky ones. In their book, it was the benefactors not the beneficiaries who were to be envied.

(c) The surprising spirituality of their giving

They did not do as we expected, but they gave themselves first to the Lord and then to us in keeping with God's will (8:5).

Paul had expected a purely pragmatic response to his appeal. 'How much is in the budget, Mr Treasurer? Are there any big bills to pay this month? How much can we afford?' But the Macedonian attitude was quite different. He says it quite took him by surprise. Instead of the calculated thriftiness of an accountant, they had demonstrated the almost irrational extravagance of a lover. It was not just money they were contributing; it was themselves. It was not just the church in Jerusalem they gave to, says Paul, it was the Lord.

This was no frigid act of bureaucratic philanthropy. There was a warmth of personal consecration infusing the act of giving. 'Jesus wants us to do this for him,' they said to one another. It was Christ-centred spirituality that motivated both the extravagance of their generosity and the cheerful willingness of it.

'That is how the churches here in Macedonia have given,' says Paul. 'And it is because we have been so encouraged by them that we are sending Titus back to you believers in Corinth with this letter in his hand, and our request that you now make available to us the funds you set apart for this important relief programme.' Let us prove to everybody, he says, that Corinth not only talks big when it comes to giving, but acts big too. 'After all,' he reminds them, 'you have a lot going for you. Compared with the Macedonian churches you are bursting with talent and resources. Make sure that in your ambition to be in the top league as regards preaching and evangelism, you do not overlook this other vital aspect of Christian living.'

> **Just as you excel in everything – in faith, in speech, in knowledge, in complete earnestness and in your love for us – see that you also excel in this grace of giving** (8:7).

It does not take great imagination to recognise the very direct challenge that these verses present to us. If the Macedonian example ought to have been a spur to affluent first-century Corinth, how much more should it be a spur to affluent twentieth-century Britain! I fear that for us too, giving is often the neglected grace in our Christian lives.

How *sacrificial* is *our* giving? I am reminded of the story of the cow and the pig who were debating who was the most generous. The cow pointed to all the pints of milk in the supermarket: 'There,' she said, 'beat that!' The pig pointed to a side of bacon. 'Your milk just represents a contribution,' he said. 'But what I give represents a sacrifice!'

Do we actually miss what we give? John Wesley learned as a young man that he could live on £28 a year. As he got older his salary grew larger, but he saw no reason to increase his standard of living; he lived perfectly adequately on £28 a year. So he just gave the surplus away. He continued living on £28 a year for the rest of his life. He gave away thousands of pounds from the sale of his books alone. How sacrificial is *our* giving? Do we know anything about Macedonian generosity?

How *enthusiastic* is *our* giving? Does resentment sometimes overcome us when the offertory bag is put in front of us, or those little envelopes come through the letter box? Some Christians give beyond their means; some Christians give according to their means; and some Christians give according to their meanness!

But supremely, how *spiritual* is *our* giving? That is the challenge of these Macedonians. First, they gave themselves to the Lord. Christian giving is not just an act of charity such as a humanist might engage in. It is an act of worship; that is why we include it in our services. It is a response to who God is and to what he has done for us.

In the Old Testament they could bring no unholy gold into the temple. In the same way, we must sanctify our money before we offer it. And the sanctification God requires of us is that first we give ourselves to him. Our giving must be a sign of Christian discipleship; not the grudging, reluctant giving of a Scrooge; nor the careless, arbitrary giving of a prodigal. Christian giving is the cheerful, thankful, prayerful giving of a consecrated disciple.

2. Giving is an expression of Christian unity (8:13-14)

> Our desire is not that others might be relieved while you are hard pressed, but that there might be equality. At the present time your plenty will supply what they need, so that in turn their plenty will supply what you need. Then there will be equality.

You may be familiar with the words of Karl Marx, 'From each according to his ability; to each according to his need.' Many commentators have pointed out how similar are Paul's sentiments in these verses. Indeed some would argue, on this basis, that every Christian should be a socialist.

I have to say that while I have some personal sympathy for socialist values, it is an overstatement to identify it here. Quite clearly Paul is talking about the free exercise of Christian charity, not the compulsory confiscation of wealth by an ecclesiastical politburo. Again and again he stresses that the contributions he seeks are entirely a matter of private conscience and decision. That was how the Macedonians had given. They had made up their minds 'entirely on their own,' (verse 3). That is how he wants the Corinthians to give too (9:7). Everybody should give what they 'decide in their heart', not 'under compulsion'. There is no coercion here then. Paul is even a trifle embarrassed at applying pressure: 'I am not commanding you' (verse 8); 'Here is my advice ... ' (verse 10). He is going out of his way to soften any suggestion that he is laying down the law in this matter.

Yet it has to be said that Paul was a socialist in one respect. He believed passionately that Christian believers should not see themselves as isolated individuals, but as having a mutual responsibility toward one another. He may not have believed in communism, but he did believe in communion – the communion of the saints. For him that was not an esoteric doctrine about our relationships with the disembodied spirits of Christians who have gone before. The communion of saints for Paul was a very practical doctrine about our relationship with materially needy Christians who were still very much here on earth. Paul makes that explicit with a word that he uses twice in these chapters, and which epitomises his social awareness. On both occasions, in the New International Version it is rendered 'sharing'. But the Greek word is *koinonia*, which in many other contexts we would translate 'fellowship' or 'communion'. That is what the Christian church is meant to be: a fellowship, a communion, a group of people glued together by a common life. And it is clear from Paul's use of the word in these chapters that Christian communion quite definitely had economic implications (8:4; 9:13).

Giving, for Paul, is not just a private Christian virtue; it is an expression of our corporate Christian unity, and never more so than, as in 8:13-14, when it is offered in a spirit of mutual aid.

Our desire is not that others might be relieved while you are hard pressed, but that there might be equality (8:13).

Equality is a loaded word these days. It is important to rid our minds of the kind of preconceptions that attach themselves to it. Paul is not arguing for a philosophy of total economic egalitarianism, although he has often been interpreted as doing so. He is not suggesting a redistribution of property to bring about precise economic parity between the Corinthians and the people in Jerusalem.

What he *is* asking for is a sharing of the Corinthians' surplus in order to eliminate the acute deprivation in Jerusalem. It was an equality in the lack of basic human need that he was campaigning for, not an equality in the absolute standard of living they enjoyed. To put it another way, there is all the difference in the world between Jesus' moral challenge to the man who has two shirts to give one to the person who has no shirt at all, and the egalitarianism that wants to confiscate a shirt from the rich man who has ten shirts in order to give it to the less rich man who has eight shirts, so they both have nine. It is economic needs Paul wants to eliminate here, not the phenomenon of economic diversity in a generally affluent society.

Furthermore, he is not arguing for an ethic of distributive justice, although again in the twentieth-century the verse has often been used to support such thinking. Paul is not suggesting that there is anything essentially immoral in the fact that the Corinthians seem to have more than their brethren in Jerusalem. That would only have been the case if the Corinthians' financial advantage was the result of exploitation on their part; and there is no hint of any such thing. In fact, we observe, as we read the New Testament, that there were considerable discrepancies of personal wealth and status in the early church; masters and slaves sat together around the same communion table. But nowhere in the New Testament do we find arguments that such economic stratification is of itself unfair. So though we may be tempted to read socialist concepts into this word 'equality', it is very important that we interpret it in the context in which Paul sets it. He is not arguing for a socialist economic philosophy; he is arguing for mutual aid.

> **At the present time your plenty will supply what they need, so that in turn their plenty will supply what you need. Then there will be equality (8:14).**

One commentator suggests that a better word might be 'equilibrium' rather than 'equality' to convey Paul's precise meaning. He is simply saying that in the fellowship of the Christian church there should be such a mutual concern for one another that seeks to meet one another's needs.

It works both ways, Paul tells us; the time may come when the boot is on the other foot and the saints in Jerusalem will be taking up a fund to relieve the saints in Corinth. It is not a question of egalitarian political doctrine or even of social justice; it is simply a question of fellowship. The people of God functions as a caring family.

> **He who gathered much did not have too much, and he that gathered little did not have too little (8:15).**

There were limits to the prosperity of the people of God that prevented the poor from being destitute and the rich from becoming greedy. Verse 15 is actually a reference to the way the Jews in the wilderness were fed by manna from heaven. One of the supernatural aspects of the manna was that you could not acquire a surplus of it. Whether you collected frugally or greedily, when they got home everybody found they had as much as they needed. That, says Paul, ought to be a model for the church's enjoyment of wealth. God gives enough for everyone but sometimes we have to do some mutual sharing to make sure that nobody goes hungry.

And that is what this relief fund is all about, he says: it is an example of the kind of mutual aid that expresses our unity in the communion of the saints. Even if we are sceptical about a welfare state, as Christians we have no right to be sceptical about a welfare church.

This is of enormous relevance to us in our churches today. Some of us have large salaries, far larger than we really need to sustain a moderate standard of living. But there are others who genuinely find it hard to make ends meet. Some are out of work; some are one-parent families; some are elderly folk living on a pension with no other source of income; some have simply been called to a job which does not remunerate them very highly. Those of us who have big salaries have a responsibility to identify those who are in need and to help them. That is what Paul means by 'equality'. It is not a question of encouraging the parasitic attitude of welfare dependency. It is an expression of the fellowship which we ought to feel within the family of God.

Indeed, I would go further. What Paul is saying here has implications beyond the walls of our local churches. The particular charitable enterprise Paul is talking about here is not Corinthian wealthy people relieving Corinthian poor people; it is the church of Corinth as a whole, living in an affluent society, seeking to relieve the poverty of a church hundreds of miles away, the faces of which they do not know. It was, if you like, 'alien poverty'; poverty that is quite detached and removed from the world of the Corinthians, except that it is the poverty of fellow-Christians.

That is very remarkable, and it ought to be an enormous challenge to us. In my own church we entertain some reservations about the modern ecumenical movement; we are disturbed by the lack of commitment it seems to show to fundamental Christian truth. It worries us that the World Council of Churches supports such liberal theologies, that it organises joint services of worship with non-Christian religions, that generally speaking it seems to show far more interest in radical politics than in evangelism or mission. As a result we have often felt it necessary as a church to stand apart from some of its attempted expressions of Christian unity which lacked, we felt, real biblical warrant and priorities. I do not regret that stand at all. I am quite prepared to defend it. But Paul is telling us here in this passage that we must not allow our dissatisfaction with the ecumenical movement to prevent us from taking bold ecumenical initiatives of our own.

For that is what this fund was: it was an exercise in inter-church cooperation. Giving is a very obvious place where such cooperation can begin. In my church, we have considerable financial potential and I do not believe that the offering we take up every Sunday represents a quarter of what we could give if we were sufficiently motivated. Of course, the question people ask is, 'Why should we give more? We meet our bills, we pay our pastor, we support our missionaries; we do not need any more money. So why give more?'

The answer is – not for ourselves truly. But there are many hundreds of thousands of Christians in this world hampered by lack of funds. They have no pastor, they cannot afford to pay one; they have no chapel, they cannot afford to build one. Some have no food because they cannot afford to buy any. Our surplus giving potential is for them. That is why God has given it to us . We owe it to those who belong to us in the international family of God's people to share with them the good things that God gives us.

> **You will be made rich in every way so that you can be generous on every occasion, and through us your generosity will result in thanksgiving to God. This service that you perform is not only supplying the needs of God's people but is also overflowing in many expressions of thanks to God. Because of the service by which you have proved yourselves, men will praise God for the obedience that accompanies your confession of the gospel of Christ, and for your generosity in sharing with them and with everyone else. And in their prayers for you their hearts will go out to you, because of the surpassing grace God has given you (9:11-14).**

Paul uses the word 'service' often to describe the charitable enterprise he is talking about. One of the chief benefits, he says, of this giving is that as an act of service it will foster relationships in the family of God. Look what is going to happen as the result of your generosity. Lots of people are going to be very grateful. They are going to be praising God for the way your generosity has helped them. They are not going to have any doubts about the authenticity of your Christian commitment. They are going to be praying for you; praying for you in a way they would never have prayed for you before, praying out of real heart-involvement because of this link of fellowship that your giving has provided.

3. Christians should give because of Christmas (8:9; 9:15)

> **For you know the grace of our Lord Jesus Christ, that though he was rich, yet for your sakes he became poor, so that you through his poverty might become rich (8:9).**
>
> **Thanks be to God for his indescribable gift (9:15).**

These verses are little jewels that shine all the more radiantly because they are set in such a prosaic argument about giving. In 8:9 we have an entire sermon on *the pre-existence of Christ* in a single phrase. 'He was rich', from all eternity he had been enthroned in the magnificence of heavenly glory. And we have *the incarnation of Christ*, once again not spelled out in theological detail, but encapsulated in a single metaphor: 'he became poor'. He took to himself something that in all eternity he had never known before: poverty. Here too is *the grace of Christ* expressed with an eloquent simplicity perhaps unrivalled in the whole of the New Testament: 'So that you through his poverty might become rich'. That is why he condescended to suffer such monumental humiliation. That is the significance of that manger in Bethlehem. He came to enrich us.

This is the grace, the *generosity* of Christ. This is Christmas. People who understand that this is what Christmas is all about cannot help but be generous themselves. Of course Christmas is a time for giving; it has to be. It is a time for emulating, no matter how feebly, the unspeakable generosity of God's gift.

There is a legend that in the fourth century, in Turkey, there was a bishop; an old man, but very saintly. One Christmas he wanted very much to show his gratitude to God for the gift of Jesus. So he went to a slum area of the city, carrying a heavy sack on his back. He knocked on the door of one of the little mud houses and was greeted by the dirty faces of three juvenile urchins. He took the pack off his back, and gave to those children a warm woollen robe each, then disappeared back to his own home. The bishop was Nicholas of Myra, and the legend of St Nicholas, though it has been commercialised as most things about Christmas are today, still has a beautiful lesson to teach. He knew the grace of the Lord Jesus who, though he was rich, became poor, and in his thankfulness he imitated him. That is the greatest reason of all for Christian giving.

It is a mark of Christian discipleship. For that reason, do not let it become a neglected grace in your life. Just as we seek to excel in all the other aspects of our Christian character and work, let us make sure we excel in this grace of giving too.

It is a wonderful expression of Christian unity; no act of service we can do for one another generates such a warmth of Christian affection and mutual prayer.

But supremely, giving is Christmas. Let us remember that, when the envelopes come through the letter box and the collecting boxes are rattled under our noses next December. Christmas is a time for saying thank you to God for his inexpressible gift, and there is no better way of doing that than by becoming givers ourselves.

10

The Wimp who Conquered Continents
(2 Corinthians 10:1-18)

By the meekness and gentleness of Christ, I appeal to you – I, Paul, who am "timid" when face to face with you, but "bold" when away! I beg you that when I come I may not have to be as bold as I expect to be toward some people who think that we live by the standards of this world. For though we live in the world, we do not wage war as the world does. The weapons we fight with are not the weapons of the world. On the contrary, they have divine power to demolish strongholds. We demolish arguments and every pretension that sets itself up against the knowledge of God, and we take captive every thought to make it obedient to Christ. And we will be ready to punish every act of disobedience, once your obedience is complete.

You are looking only on the surface of things. If anyone is confident that he belongs to Christ, he should consider again that we belong to Christ just as much as he. For even if I boast somewhat freely about the authority the Lord gave us for building you up rather than pulling you down, I will not be ashamed of it. I do not want to seem to be trying to frighten you with my letters. For some say, "His letters are weighty and forceful, but in person he is unimpressive and his speaking amounts to nothing." Such people should realize that what we are in our letters when we are absent, we will be in our actions when we are present.

We do not dare to classify or compare ourselves with some who commend themselves. When they measure themselves by themselves and compare themselves with themselves, they are not wise. We, however, will not boast beyond proper limits, but will confine our boasting to the field God has assigned to us, a field that reaches even to you. We are not going too far in our boasting, as would be the case if we had not come to you, for we did get as far as you with the gospel of Christ. Neither do we go beyond our limits by boasting of work done by others. Our hope is that, as your faith continues to grow, our area of activity among you will greatly expand, so that we can preach the gospel in the regions beyond you. For we do not want to boast about work already done in another man's territory. But, "Let him who boasts boast in the Lord." For it is not the one who commends himself who is approved, but the one whom the Lord commends (2 Corinthians 10:1-18).

IT IS SAID THAT YOU CAN TELL THE QUALITY OF A PERSON BY THE COMPANY THEY KEEP. But I want to suggest to you an even better index of human character: you can tell the quality of a person by the people they admire.

You cannot always be selective about your company. Sometimes, good manners or family duty or sheer economic necessity force us to associate in our neighbourhood, home or workplace with people whom we would frankly rather avoid. Much as we might like to, we cannot always choose our circle of acquaintance. But admiration is a tribute that lies wholly in our own discretion. We choose our heroes. Nobody chooses them for us. We choose them because they enshrine the kind of qualities to which we aspire. We magnify them because in some way they personify our own ambitions and dreams. We esteem them because in our secret fantasies, at least, we wish we could be like them. That is why you can tell the quality of a person by the people they admire. Tell me the subjects of your favourite biographies, the names of your favourite pin-ups on the bedroom wall, your champions, your stars, the person you would most like to meet; and I will tell you a lot about yourself.

The Christians at Corinth were in division and confusion precisely because they could not make up their minds about whom they wanted to admire. On the one hand there was Paul, the apostle who had founded their church and for whom many inevitably held a great respect because he was the one who had led them to Christ. But on the other hand, there was a group of newcomers in the congregation, they also called themselves apostles but were altogether different from Paul. They were not shy about parading their contempt for him, as we have already seen in previous chapters. 'What do you want to admire him for?' they demanded. 'There are others far more worthy of your esteem. Us, for instance!'

So the Corinthians found themselves caught between rival claimants for their respect, and as a result loyalty swung wildly in the congregation. First Paul was in the limelight, and then the other group captured it from him. If the office of apostleship had been decided by popular vote, then the opinion pollsters would have had a marvellous time trying to predict the outcome of this particular by-election. Corinth could not make up its mind whom it admired, and in a quite startling way, these final chapters of Paul's letter to them reflect that violent oscillation of mood.

You will remember that in the earlier part of this epistle, though Paul has been very aware of the presence of a rival faction in Corinth, the general tone of his writing has been optimistic. In Chapter 7, in fact, he was so reassured by the good news Titus had brought him that he was almost euphoric. But we do not have to go very far into Chapters 10-13 before we detect an altogether more pessimistic outlook. Paul seems in these chapters to be more on the defensive than ever. Both in the bitter severity of his warnings and in the emotional intensity of his appeals, he seems to give evidence of a man who is fighting tooth and nail not just for his reputation as an apostle, but for his recognition as a Christian.

How are we to explain this sudden change of tone, and the dramatic loss of confidence in the Corinthians that it seems to indicate? Some argue that we should not exaggerate it: that Paul is simply turning his guns directly on to the opposition party in these final four chapters. Whereas in earlier chapters he was softening up the congregation as a whole, now he is giving his enemies a full broadside, and that is why he talks so differently. But most commentators feel that the mood swing is too sudden and too marked for that, and I am inclined to agree with them that some additional explanation is required.

Perhaps following Titus' arrival somebody else turned up from Corinth, giving Paul more depressing information on how things were going there which forced him to add this urgent postscript to his letter before he sent it off? Or maybe Chapters 10-13 are actually another letter altogether, which some editor has tacked on the end of 2 Corinthians for convenience; that is quite possible too. Some commentators even argue that these chapters comprise the earlier, so-called 'severe letter', which Paul has mentioned in previous chapters.

As is so often the case in matters like this, we can only speculate.

But one thing is certain. The Paul who wrote the last four chapters of 2 Corinthians is not the buoyant, sanguine, reassured Paul who wrote Chapters 1 to 9. Something has changed. He is anxious, perhaps almost a little desperate. The opposition party is being given far too sympathetic a hearing at Corinth, and Paul feels that he must do something about it. He is not motivated by personal pique: it would be quite wrong to think that Paul's hard line in these four chapters simply reflects a sulky resentment that the Corinthians should be so fickle in their loyalty. Far more is at stake than that. Paul knows that he is confronting here not just a minority faction of disenchanted church members who dislike him, but a self-styled spiritual élite intent on commending a radically new model of Christian spirituality to the believers in Corinth.

What sort of apostles did Corinth want? What sort of Christians did Corinth admire? That was the issue and it was no small matter. For it was not just a question of petty personal rivalries. The people we admire are the people we want to be. The kind of Christianity that the church lionises is the kind of Christianity that the church is going to reflect. It matters who our Christian heroes are; that is why God chooses his heroes so carefully.

> By the meckness and gentleness of Christ, I appeal to you – I, Paul, who am 'timid' when face to face with you, but 'bold' when away! I beg you that when I come I may not have to be as bold as I expect to be towards some people, who think that we live by the standards of this world (10:1-2).

The newspapers often provide dramatic evidence of how difficult and embarrassing it can be for a public figure to be subjected to a conspiracy of uncorroborated allegation and innuendo. It is not easy in such circumstances to clear one's name. And Paul is experiencing the same kind of helpless frustration. It is very difficult to defend yourself against a smear campaign; often the very act of trying simply gives more opportunity to your detractors.

It is clear that Paul has been accused of being a cowardly bully who is very good at writing domineering letters. They said that in person he was a craven weakling, an ineffectual wimp. But he had megalomaniac pretensions: a timid puppy who barked like a 'bold' rottweiller from behind the fence!

"His letters are weighty and forceful, but in person he is unimpressive and his speaking amounts to nothing" (10:10).

How do you write a letter to counter such a charge without playing into your critics' hands? Whatever tone you adopt, they can twist it to their own advantage. If you play it strong or weak, they will only say you are confirming their point.

Paul's answer is to take the wind out of their sails at the outset by appealing to a Christian hero whom even his rivals could not impeach. 'By the meekness and gentleness of Christ,' he says, 'I appeal to you.'

The whole debate was really about styles of Christian leadership. Paul's rivals said he was not dynamic or forceful enough – 'Well,' said Paul, 'I will tell you right from the start what my leadership model is: the meekness, the gentleness of Christ.' The moderation and mildness they have observed in Paul, and which they called timidity, is simply his attempt to emulate the graciousness of his Master. Perhaps the imitation is imperfect, but it is considerably better than some he could mention! How much, for instance, do those would-be apostles in their midst display a likeness to the one who said of himself, 'I am meek and lowly in heart'? Where does *that* kind of Christ-like humility fit into their catalogue of Christian heroics?

As they read these final chapters they were going to find him saying some firm, harsh things. 'Some will no doubt say I am just being my usual inconsistent self, writing strong letters as a smokescreen to mask the weakness of my personality,' says Paul. 'Well, I want you to realise that I do not desire to lay the law down like some ecclesiastical tyrant. Whenever I have been with you, you know I have done my best to be mild-mannered and non-intimidating, because that is what Jesus was like.'

It is completely out of character, Paul insists, for him to play the spiritual heavyweight. If they detect a change of mood in these chapters, they must understand that it is a most reluctant one. They have forced him to it. He dislikes playing the role of a Christian superstar, whatever his enemies may say. Apostleship is no ego-trip for Paul. He has no power complex. On the contrary, his model of spiritual leadership is 'the meekness and gentleness of Christ'. And for that reason, his greatest wish is that when he comes to Corinth he will not have to play an authoritarian role at all. He wants to sort things out in advance, so that he can display the kind of tenderness towards them that he would like. But they must realise that, just as Jesus, the meek and lowly one, could on occasion make a whip and drive the worldly moneychangers out of his Father's temple, so he, Paul, could, if the occasion demanded, exert his apostolic authority against these slanderous impostors in their midst and with equal severity drive them out of the church. 'Do not mistake my meekness for weakness,' he warns.

> **Though we live in the world, we do not wage war as the world does. The weapons we fight with are not the weapons of the world. On the contrary, they have divine power to demolish strongholds. We demolish arguments and every pretension that sets itself up against the knowledge of God, and we take captive every thought to make it obedient to Christ. And we will be ready to punish every act of disobedience, once your obedience is complete (10:3-6).**

Paul's critics accuse him of living by the standards of the world (verse 2, literally, 'of the flesh'). That is, his spirituality is suspect, he has no evidence of divine charisma in his ministry, there is no supernatural power in him. They call him an old windbag, full of words, a craven dog who barks loudly, but has no teeth when it comes to face-to-face confrontation. 'I know what they say about me,' says Paul. 'Well, let me tell you, I have got all the teeth I need to settle those so-called apostles of yours.'

What kind of divine power is Paul claiming, that is going to enable him to punish this Corinthian disobedience? Is he threatening some kind of supernatural vengeance on his enemies? That is not impossible, for in the book of Acts we are told how Ananias and Sapphira were struck dead after an act of church discipline by Peter (Acts 5). On another occasion a pagan sorcerer called Elymas was blinded when Paul denounced him as a demonic liar (Acts 13). So the authority of the apostles was sometimes supported in the New Testament by miraculous acts of divine judgment; and Paul may well have anticipated some such intervention at Corinth. Alternatively he may be merely anticipating a court of inquisition, with himself presiding over the judicial excommunication of offending church members. It is known that such discipline was imposed by the early church, and we find clear evidence that such proceedings were in view at Corinth later on in Chapter 13.

But the thrust of these verses seems to suggest that the apostolic power that Paul has primarily in mind – and which he is threatening to use – is that of Spirit-inspired words. 'The weapons we fight with ... have divine power to demolish ... arguments and every pretension that sets itself up against the knowledge of God, and we take captive every thought to make it obedient to Christ' (verses 4-5). These are military metaphors. Paul is imagining himself in combat against titanic forces: the proud fortresses of human speculation, the vast army of demonically-inspired ideas that challenge his gospel. 'Coward though I am supposed to be,' says Paul, 'I am more than a match for such opponents.'

What an encouragement Paul's success in the ideological contest for the hearts and minds of people should be to us. We too must engage aggressively with secular thought and refuse to be intimidated by it.

Notice the implications of Paul's words here:

First, he says that *we are meant to live 'in the world'*. I suspect his rivals may have questioned that. As we have seen, they may well have been campaigning for a more esoteric Christianity that favoured a retreat into the otherworldly security of a mystery cult. They certainly complained that Paul was not 'spiritual' enough. But Paul insists that it is not the Christian's role to detach himself from the world by putting on some aloof, holy, super-spiritual image. We live in the world and that is where we are meant to live. Our gospel is about an incarnate Saviour and it has to be preached by an incarnate church.

Second, he says that *we do not use the world's methods.* The 'weapons' of the world that Paul is thinking about here are the sophisticated rhetoric which these rivals of his at Corinth special-ised in and valued so much. Christians, says Paul, ought not to employ that kind of religious showmanship. He eschewed the rhetoric of the orator, the sophistication of the philosopher, the mystique of the priesthood. He created no artificial atmospheres, he projected no personality cult, he exploited no gimmicks. For he relied on spiritual weapons: the weapons of prayer and personal holiness, the Spirit of Christ, and the Word of God.

Third, *with those spiritual weapons he conquered continents.*

> **We demolish arguments and every pretension that sets itself up against the knowledge of God, and we take captive every thought to make it obedient to Christ** (10:5).

Don't those words excite you? Paul had supreme confidence in the superiority of the gospel over its intellectual rivals. He really be-lieved that it was possible to conquer contemporary secular ideas by a courageous wielding of the sword of Christian truth. So when people contradicted his gospel, he didn't retreat. No matter how strong the enemy position seemed to be, he was sure his apostolic message could demolish it. He saw the intellectual opinions and philosophical systems of the world as towers of Babel, arrogant structures built by the sinful imaginations of men in defiance of the authority of God. And it was his job to challenge those proud fortresses of human independence.

Paul was not content simply to knock down non-Christian argu-ments. He wanted to captivate his opponent, not humiliate him. Anybody can win a battle of words, but silencing somebody is not the same as convincing them. Paul wanted to see the minds of his non-Christian hearers not just overwhelmed with superior logic, but changed; not simply confuted, but converted.

That was his ambition. He knew that Christian truth had divine power to do it; to bring rebel minds into voluntary submission to the Lord Jesus Christ. And, again and again he had demonstrated that divine power in his apostolic ministry.

Why, Paul had dealt with pagan wizards, Roman proconsuls and Athenian philosophers in his time, not to mention a few lynch-mobs. Did the Corinthians really think that a handful of silver-tongued pseudo-apostles was going to be a problem to him? 'I appeal to you,' he begs, 'do not force me into the unwelcome role of a disciplinarian. By the meekness and gentleness of Christ, I beg you to spare me the pain of having to prove to you just how powerful an apostle of Jesus Christ I can be when the situation demands it.' After all, for someone who is supposed to be so 'worldly', I have been extraordinarily successful in conquering the 'world' for Christ!'

> **And we will be ready to punish every act of disobedience, once your obedience is complete** (10:6).

In other words, when Paul arrives in Corinth, his first priority will be to establish his apostolic authority in the church as a whole. That done, he will have absolutely no trouble in court-marshalling these rebel leaders in the Corinthian camp, for clever and eloquent though they may be, he will trounce them. He is certain of it. The superficiality and spuriousness of their ideas are going to be undeniably exposed, and in the strength of the victory Paul will win over them, like Elijah of old he will purge the church of the error that has infiltrated it. 'Oh,' he says, 'I know what you will say! There he goes again, windbag Paul, trying to intimidate us all with threatening letters. Pay no attention to his hectoring; he is just sabre-rattling, trying to demoralise us for his own ends. His bark is worse than his bite; his letters are weighty and forceful, but as a person he is unimpressive and his speaking amounts to nothing' (verse 10).

But if that is what his critics are saying, Paul tells the Corinthi-ans, they are wrong on three counts. They are wrong first of all because they *misjudge* him.

> **You are looking only on the surface of things. If anyone is confident that he belongs to Christ, he should consider again that we belong to Christ just as much as he** (10:7).

In other words, 'If you looked at things a little less superficially, you would quickly realise there is a lot more Christianity in me than your friends make out.'

Secondly, he says, they are wrong because they *misrepresent* him.

> **Even if I boast somewhat freely about the authority the Lord gave us for building you up rather than pulling you down, I will not be ashamed of it** (10:8)

'All right,' says Paul, 'I do claim spiritual authority; I admit it. I have a right to do so. The Lord has given me that authority for your good, and anybody who suggests that I have anything other than your best interests at heart is a liar.'

But thirdly, says Paul, they are wrong because they *underestimate* him.

> **Such people should realise that what we are in our letters when we are absent, we will be in our actions when we are present** (10:11).

'Do not be fooled by the unimpressive exterior,' warns Paul; 'my letters faithfully mirror the person I am. Let nobody think that I am incapable of translating my words into actions! And if you are disposed not to believe me on that,' challenges Paul, 'just examine my record. Consider the way that God has used me in other places in the past.'

> **We do not dare to classify or compare ourselves with some who commend themselves. When they measure themselves by themselves and compare themselves with themselves, they are not wise. We, however, will not boast beyond proper limits** (10:12-13a).

It is difficult to convey the biting note of sarcasm in these words, without some kind of paraphrasing. J. B. Phillips gets quite near it: 'Of course, we shouldn't dare to include ourselves in the same class as those who write their own testimonials. We shouldn't even dare to compare ourselves with them.'

Paul here is exploiting a very obvious chink in his opponents' armour, which we have already observed: that their authority rested entirely on self-congratulation. They had turned up on the Corinthians' doorstep with no credentials except their own glib tongues and some fancy letters of reference written by members of their own little party. 'Can you not see the folly of this little mutual admiration society?' asks Paul.

> **When they measure themselves by themselves and compare themselves with themselves, they are not wise. We, however, will not boast beyond proper limits, but will confine our boasting to the field God has assigned to us ... (10:12b-13).**

In other words, Paul unlike them is not in the business of making wild, uncorroborated claims for himself. There is a limit set by God himself to the kind of boasting he engages in and the kind of authority he asserts, and it is a limit confirmed by the objective evidence of his own ministry.

The word translated 'field' means literally a 'measure', but by extension it could mean a measured area, like a field or the lane of a running track. Its use here imparts a double meaning to the paragraph. On one hand Paul seems to be referring to the division of labour agreed between him and Peter in the early days of the missionary expansion. Paul said he would go north-west into the Greek-speaking areas of Europe and Asia; he was recognised as apostle to the Gentiles. Peter would supervise developments around Jerusalem. 'I have stuck to my field,' says Paul, 'to the area that God has assigned me to. I do not exert authority outside it.'

On the other hand, he is making a more general point: that if you are going to boast about something you had better make sure you have objective and 'measurable' evidence to back up your boasting.

It is all too easy to brag, but a wise man does not claim more than he can substantiate. 'If I boast at all,' says Paul, 'I boast about things that can be undeniably proven by observation of my ministry.'

On both counts, Paul is in a far stronger position than his rivals. Firstly, because Corinth was in his field; it was part of his apostolic diocese. His rivals had no right to exert authority there. Secondly, because his record of missionary labour clearly confirmed his apostolic calling. He had been successful as a missionary; his claims could be substantiated by the number of souls saved and churches planted. 'Put the measuring rule alongside me,' says Paul. 'There is concrete evidence.'

> **We are not going too far in our boasting, as would be the case if we had not come to you, for we did get as far as you with the gospel of Christ. Neither do we go beyond our limits by boasting of work done by others. Our hope is that, as your faith continues to grow, our area of activity among you will greatly expand, so that we can preach the gospel in the regions beyond you. For we do not want to boast about work already done in another man's territory (10:14-16).**

You see the point he is trying to make. He, Paul, evangelised the people at Corinth; he planted the church there, and his hope is that the work will be consolidated so that he can use it as a launching pad to further pioneer outreach in the western part of the Roman empire. The so-called apostles in their midst have to rely on self-praise because that is all they have; they have no such record as Paul's of successful church planting to their credit. They are interlopers trying to poach his patch. If they had a real apostolic calling then they would be, like Paul, out doing front-line missionary work in their own allotted zone. But they are just parasites, seeking to exploit the labours of others to their own advantage. In exasperation Paul turns again to irony: no, he would not be so presumptuous as to aspire to their lofty company; boasting of somebody else's evangelistic achievement is beyond even his humble reach!

> **For we do not want to boast about work already done in another man's territory. But, 'Let him who boasts boast in the Lord.' For it is not the one who commends himself who is approved, but the one whom the Lord commends (10:16-18).**

If only the Corinthians had been a little less dazzled by the glossy image and looked a little more carefully beneath the surface, they would realise that their so-called apostles had not been commended by the Lord at all. 'But,' says Paul, 'I have: look at my record, it speaks for itself. Maybe I look unimpressive. Maybe my public speaking lacks professional polish. Maybe my manner seems weak and unassertive. '

But you must not underestimate Paul. For God had used him to conquer continents – yes, even Paul the 'timid', Paul the wimp!

So what sort of Christian do we admire? Speaking personally, I admire Christians who, like Paul, choose to go to the hard places where pioneer evangelism is the order of the day. I admire Christians who, like Paul, are thinking of the next challenge to their ministry and who are not resting on their laurels, boasting of their past achievements. I admire Christians who, like Paul, rely on the spiritual weapons of prayer, holiness and preaching to get their evangelism done, and eschew the gimmicks of secular showmanship.

I admire Christians who, like Paul, believe in the power of Christian truth to change the world; who refuse to be intimidated by advocates of error, no matter how daunting their power-base seems to be. I admire Christians like Paul who hate talking about themselves or throwing their spiritual weight around. I admire Christians who, like Paul, do not take their model of Christian greatness from the glossy world of entertainment or politics, but who make their boast in the Lord, and draw their inspiration from the meekness and gentleness of Christ.

That is my kind of Christian hero.

What sort of Christian do you admire? For I tell you, the kind of Christian you admire will be the kind of Christian you will become.

11

The Amateur who Fathered Churches
(2 Corinthians 11:1-15)

I hope you will put up with a little of my foolishness; but you are already doing that. I am jealous for you with a godly jealousy. I promised you to one husband, to Christ, so that I might present you as a pure virgin to him. But I am afraid that just as Eve was deceived by the serpent's cunning, your minds may somehow be led astray from your sincere and pure devotion to Christ. For if someone comes to you and preaches a Jesus other than the Jesus we preached, or if you receive a different spirit from the one you received, or a different gospel from the one you accepted, you put up with it easily enough. But I do not think I am in the least inferior to those "super apostles". I may not be a trained speaker, but I do have knowledge. We have made this perfectly clear to you in every way.

Was it a sin for me to lower myself in order to elevate you by preaching the gospel of God to you free of charge? I robbed other churches by receiving support from them so as to serve you. And when I was with you and needed something, I was not a burden to anyone, for the brothers who came from Macedonia supplied what I needed. I have kept myself from being a burden to you in any way, and will continue to do so. As surely as the truth of Christ is in me, nobody in the regions of Achaia will stop this boasting of mine. Why? Because I do not love you? God knows I do! And I will keep on doing what I am doing in order to cut the ground from under those who want an opportunity to be considered equal with us in the things they boast about.

For such men are false apostles, deceitful workmen, masquerading as apostles of Christ. And no wonder, for Satan himself masquerades as an angel of light. It is not surprising, then, if his servants masquerade as servants of righteousness. Their end will be what their actions deserve (2 Corinthians 11:1-15).

IT HAS BEEN SAID THAT SARCASM IS THE LOWEST FORM OF WIT. That may be so, but I suspect that there are times when it is a legitimate form of self-defence. Certainly the apostle Paul felt so, because these last final chapters of 2 Corinthians abound in it.

Understandably, the gibes and allegations of his critics hurt Paul deeply. So it is not surprising that in replying to their attack he sometimes lets his wounded feelings show by the bitter edge he gives to his tongue. In fact you could say that he had no alternative but to respond in such tones, because the whole situation was a crazy paradox. Here was he, a true apostle of Jesus Christ, being accused by false apostles, of being a false apostle himself! It was a bitterly ironic situation.

> **I hope you will put up with a little of my foolishness; but you are already doing that** (11:1).

Solomon advised us to answer fools according to their folly, and that is what Paul was doing. It embarrasses him to talk about himself. To be forced into a position where he has to blow his own trumpet makes him feel a bit of an idiot. But he says, 'Since you Corinthians think I am an idiot anyway, there is nothing much to lose, is there? I am already the object of your patronising contempt, so it is not much to ask you to tolerate a little more of poor old Paul's buffoonery.' He could hardly make himself look more ridiculous in their eyes. So at the risk of making them in Corinth cripple up with laughter still further, he proposes to tell them exactly how he feels about them.

> **I am jealous for you with a godly jealousy. I promised you to one husband, to Christ, so that I might present you as a pure virgin to him. But I am afraid that just as Eve was deceived by the serpent's cunning, your minds may somehow be led astray from your sincere and pure devotion to Christ** (11:2).

As we have already seen, there is far more to these chapters than a wounded man replying to spiteful personal criticism. If all that had been at stake was Paul's good name, it is doubtful whether he would have made much fuss. After all, in one way or another he had suffered humiliation all his life; a little more from the vitriolic insinuations of these Corinthian so-called apostles was not going to make much difference to him.

But there was a much larger issue involved. This was more than mere anti-Paul propaganda. The so-called apostles were not just trying to undermine Paul's personal influence, they were trying to undermine the kind of Christianity that Paul stood for. They wanted a religion more congenial to the sophisticated, Hellenistic culture of their day. It was not just Paul's image that they found unacceptable; Christianity itself, they said, needs a face-lift. Paul makes it clear in these verses that there is something sinister, even demonic about the opposition party in Corinth. He sees them as agents of the devil, craftily seducing a virgin bride of Christ into spiritual adultery just as Eve was seduced by Satan in the garden of Eden. And Paul says that he is desperately worried about it.

'Forgive the fussy anxiety of a silly old man, if that is how you see me, but I feel I have a right to express my concern for you in this matter. After all, I am your spiritual father.' Paul had founded the church at Corinth, and as a result felt a fierce possessiveness. He is jealous for her with a godly jealousy, he says, as any father is towards his daughter. Not that he is one of those awful parents who does not want his children to grow up to adult independence; he is quite willing to give her away. He *wants* to give her away. Nobody will be prouder than Paul on her wedding day, because there is no better husband in the world than the one to whom she is betrothed: Jesus Christ. When on the last day God says, 'Who gives this church to my Son?', Paul wants to be able to say, 'I do.'

But like any father he would be utterly ashamed and humiliated should his daughter's chastity be compromised by a flirtation with some other man before that marriage ceremony takes place. And that is precisely what he fears is happening.

> For if someone comes to you and preaches a Jesus other than
> the Jesus we preached, or if you receive a different spirit
> from the one you received, or a different gospel from the one
> you accepted, you put up with it easily enough (11:4).

Do you hear the sarcasm in his voice again? 'You have more time
these days, it seems, for your spiritual gigolos, than for me your
spiritual father. You put up with them, but you will not put up with
me. Do you not realise that for all their smooth talk, these apostles
of yours are leading you astray? They represent a different gospel,
a different spirit: an alternative Jesus.'

Opinions differ about what precisely Paul is implying when he
uses that word 'different', for he uses very similar language in his
letter to the Galatians to describe a group of Jewish legalists. They
were offering 'a different gospel' too (Gal. 1:6). So some conclude
that this Corinthian faction represented the same kind of heresy, a
suggestion that gains some support from the implication that Paul
makes in verse 22, that his rivals in Corinth were indeed Aramaic-
speaking Jews. But it does have to be said, I think, that there is no
other evidence of the Galatian heresy in Corinth. Indeed, most of the
information we have suggests that the Corinthian church leaned
rather in the opposite direction, towards Hellenistic licentiousness
rather than Judaistic legalism. And if this rival party were advocating some clearly identifiable error as the Galatian heretics were,
then surely Paul would have spent some time addressing the theological issues involved. But there is in fact nothing in 2 Corinthians,
apart from these verses, to suggest that these so-called apostles were
not, superficially at any rate, orthodox in doctrine.

My own suspicion is that their very orthodoxy may well have
been why Paul saw them as such a subtle threat and felt obliged to
reply to them in the very personal way he does. Their error lay not
in specific false teaching but in their methodology, their emphases,
their leadership style. Their desire for a Christianity more congenial
to the mindset of secular Greek society demanded a gospel that
majored on strength, not weakness; in heavenly triumph, not earthly

suffering. In a word, they wanted a Christianity that played down the cross and played up the glory. For, as far as they were concerned, it was the glory that was Christianity's selling-point.

That is why Paul would not do as an apostle as far as they were concerned. Firstly, he was a weak man himself, in their judgment. And secondly, he concentrated so much in his preaching on the weakness of Jesus: his stated philosophy in Corinth was, 'I resolved to know nothing while I was with you except Jesus Christ and him crucified' (1 Cor. 2.2). How on earth could he expect to win a Greek audience to his side, with such a tasteless message of gory failure? The pseudo-apostles wanted an impressive, dynamic, strong apostle, to commend an impressive, dynamic, strong Jesus to a secular culture which had no time for weaklings and still less for victims of crucifixion.

That is why Paul said they preached a different Jesus. Not so much because of any particular truth they denied or any particular heresy they affirmed, or he would have told us about it; but because the image of Christian spirituality they projected was unbalanced. 'You are being seduced,' says Paul, 'not so much by a lie, as by a fake; by a regiment of pseudo-apostles whose lives model a pseudo-Christianity.' How were they doing it? In the same way that the serpent did it in the garden of Eden; by their glib tongues.

> I may not be a trained speaker, but I do have knowledge. We have made this perfectly clear to you in every way.
>   Was it a sin for me to lower myself in order to elevate you by preaching the gospel of God to you free of charge? (11:6-7).

One of the charges levelled at Paul in Corinth was that his public speaking lacked refinement. He did not have the style of a Greek orator; his preaching, though effective in its own way, lacked professionalism. He did not even charge a fee for it! The Greeks did not have any respect for cheap oratory.

When I lived in Africa, I encountered a similar prejudice with regard to medicine. The more expensive the medicine prescribed, the better the doctor was considered to be. I can recall several of my African friends telling me proudly how they had ignored the free drugs from the hospital in preference to the very expensive treatment offered by some (I suspect) less well-trained person, who had set himself up in a Harley Street-style practice in the big city.

Paul's rivals sought an advantage over him by precisely the same kind of professional one-upmanship. 'If he was any good, he would charge a proper fee for his services,' they said, 'like we do.' It must be said that in a sense Paul had played into their hands in this matter. For in Acts 18:3 we are told that he not only did not charge the Corinthians for his preaching, but for at least part of the time he actually earned his own living there by manual work, tent making. To a Greek, that was absolutely shameful; only slaves worked with their hands. The trouble with Paul, his detractors insisted, was that he had an inferior working-class mind. How could he be a Christian leader? He was just an amateur loudmouth, a soapbox preacher. No educated person would waste their time listening to him.

'Well,' says Paul – the sarcasm coming back into his voice – 'I reckon I am not quite so outclassed by these incomparable arch-apostles of yours as they claim. And I will give you two reasons.'

1. Paul's preaching has content, not just polish

> I may not be a trained speaker, but I do have knowledge. We have made this perfectly clear to you in every way (11:6).

By the standards of Demosthenes he may not be a great orator, but at least Paul has something to talk about. The public utterances of Paul's opponents may have been a dazzling performance by comparison, but they left people in ignorance, particularly simple people. As Disraeli said of Gladstone, they were just 'sophisticated rhetoricians, inebriated with the exuberance of their own verbosity'.

By contrast, Paul's preaching, plain and unvarnished though it may be, had at least the advantage of communicating the truth of

God to ordinary people. Unlike that of their super-apostles, his preaching informed, it did not merely dazzle. It had content, not just polish. And that is the first reason he does not think he is quite as inferior to them as they say he is.

2. Paul's motives are unselfish, not merely mercenary

> Was it a sin for me to lower myself in order to elevate you by preaching the gospel of God to you free of charge? (11:7)

There is indignation as well as sarcasm in his retort. Are they really seriously suggesting that it was a sign of his failure, that he did not exploit them financially? He should have passed the collection box more often – they would have had more respect for him if he had done that!

'You silly people!', he says. 'Don't you realise that the only reason I was able to live at Corinth at all was because Christians elsewhere, more thoughtful and appreciative than you, were voluntarily providing for my needs? I deprived other churches by receiving support from them so that I could serve you. How dare you accuse me of being a bungling apprentice in the business of preaching the gospel! The only reason you did not have to pay is that others valued my ministry so much that they were prepared to impoverish themselves for your sake!'

The inexpensiveness of Paul's ministry was no mark of amateurism. It was a carefully considered missionary policy.

> When I was with you and needed something, I was not a burden to anyone, for the brothers who came from Macedonia supplied what I needed. I have kept myself from being a burden to you in any way, and will continue to do so (11:9).

As far as Paul was concerned, it would have cheapened the gospel to have made people pay for it. He would not reduce himself to the level of a professional entertainer. He came as an ambassador of the King, not as some peddler of religious quackery. There were plenty of charlatans in the ancient world whose business was selling religion for money. But no one would ever accuse Paul of being one of them.

> **As surely as the truth of Christ is in me, nobody in the regions of Achaia will stop this boasting of mine. Why? Because I do not love you? God knows I do! And I will keep on doing what I am doing [that is, preaching the gospel free of charge] in order to cut the ground from under those who want an opportunity to be considered equal with us in the things they boast about (11:10-12).**

In other words: 'If the truth be known, these so-called super-apostles would dearly love to be able to claim the same financial independence of you that I can. They are the ones who have the inferiority complex, not me. And goad me as they may, I am not going to give up my so-called amateur status, precisely to frustrate them in their ambition to compete with me. If by some extraordinary contortion of logic they can succeed in presenting my refusal to exploit you as evidence of a lack of loving regard to you all – well, all I can say is that God knows they are wrong. In fact, they are more than wrong; they are deliberately misrepresenting me in order to mislead you. Don't you realise who you are gallivanting with? Super-apostles, my foot! The devil is never more dangerous than when he comes to young Christians like you, dressed in the garb of Christian leadership.'

> **For such men are false apostles, deceitful workmen, masquerading as apostles of Christ. And no wonder, for Satan himself masquerades as an angel of light. It is not surprising, then, if his servants masquerade as servants of righteousness. Their end will be what their actions deserve (11:13-15).**

At last the veil of sarcasm and irony is removed. Now Paul unambiguously affirms what he has so far hinted at. These so-called apostles are not just difficult or immature Christians. They are fake Christians. Their claims to divine inspiration are spurious. Deceitful workmen, they offer their services out of a desire to cheat the Corinthians. Masquerading as apostles, their pious external appearance is just a disguise to mask the malevolence of their real intentions.

'You are surprised by this?' asks Paul. 'But there is nothing very amazing about people like that. They are just taking a leaf out of the book of their master. When Satan wants to injure the church he invariably dresses himself up as a Christian, for imitation is his stock-in-trade. Originality is beyond him. His technique is always to fill the world with counterfeits that confuse and mislead people, and that is what has happened to you Corinthians. You are being so bemused by the rhetoric and so flattered by the attention of these would-be leaders in your midst that you cannot see that the kind of Christianity they are cultivating in you is different from the Christianity you have received. Like the Sirens of Greek mythology, they are luring you Corinthians away from the path of safety on to the rocks, by the simple device of a deceptive diabolical charm.'

But there are, says Paul, two distinguishing marks the devil can never eradicate from his products: their moral quality and their final destiny. Their tongues may sound spiritual, but their lives always bear the give-away trademark: 'manufactured in Hell', and one day that is where they will go. 'Their end will be what their actions deserve.'

'They may call me an amateur loudmouth: in a sense, perhaps I am,' Paul says. 'I have no pretensions to the sophistication they admire. But I am genuine: genuine in the Jesus I portray to you, genuine in the love I share with you. Amateur loudmouth – yes, I accept the gibe. But I am your spiritual father, the spiritual father of dozens of churches. I have a right to rebuke you for philandering with these spiritual snakes-in-the-grass. If my sarcasm seems bitter, it is far less bitter than the misery you will bring upon yourselves if you go on jeopardising your relationship with the real Jesus, by your flirtations with these fakes!'

It is a fierce passage, is it not? Few passages in all Paul's writings are quite so emotionally intense. And it is a passage with great practical relevance for many of us. Beware of Christian gullibility.

In 1822 a man called Smith claimed he had received a visitation from an angel. He said that this heavenly emissary, called Moroni, directed him to some gold plates hidden on a hill in Palmyra in New York State. They were inscribed with ancient Egyptian hieroglyphics, which he was enabled to read by means of a specially-provided pair of angelic spectacles. On translation, these plates revealed extraordinary facts about the early history of the American continent, not the least being that America was not discovered by Christopher Columbus but by a Jewish prophet called Lehi, 600 years before Christ, and that Christ himself appeared after his resurrection to the descendants of that ancient Jewish family in the New World. Incredible? I think so. But three million adherents of the Church of the Latter Day Saints – the Mormons, as they are called – believe it is absolutely true.

The greatest problem for the Christian church is not (as you might have thought) the rise of scientific scepticism but the growth of public gullibility. G. K. Chesterton said that when people abandon the truth, they do not believe in nothing, they believe in anything. There are thousands of cults and sects in our world today, many of which one would have thought would strain the credulity of Simple Simon by their bizarre and fantastic speculation. And all of them, by their numerical success, prove the accuracy of Chesterton's assertion. People will believe in anything.

The church does not have to worry seriously about atheism; that is an ephemeral superstition. It does not seriously threaten the religious consciousness of the world. Marxism sustained whatever limited success it had in promoting it only by vicious policies of repression. No; the real danger is not unbelief, but wrong belief; not scepticism, but superstition; not irreligion, but gullibility; not the doubter, but the deceiver. Again and again church history has proven this true. It is not external assaults on Christianity by its ideological, philosophical or religious rivals that have represented the most serious threat to its survival. It is the subtle infiltration of saboteurs who exploit the gullibility of Christian people.

They are the ones who do the damage. Saboteurs who, as often as not, present themselves as Christian ministers and succeed in duping the sheep by their false claims to spiritual authority. It is not as if we have not been warned about this. Paul told the elders of the church in Ephesus that such savage predators would arise 'from your own number'. Out of the eldership of the church you will find such people coming, distorting the truth, 'drawing away disciples after them' (Acts 20:30). Jesus spoke too of false prophets, who would come dressed in sheep's clothing, but who would be, inwardly, wolves.

The warnings are there: but the devil is clever. As the Corinthians found, the impersonation is good and the seduction is subtle. And Christians are credulous. They find it hard to believe that anybody who sounds so spiritual and looks so charming could possibly be an agent of the evil one. Beware of Christian gullibility, then. Harmless as doves we may have to be, but wise as serpents too. For it is a wily serpent we have to fight. Perhaps some observations from 2 Corinthians 11 will make us a little less gullible.

(a) Do not be fooled by words

Clearly Paul's rivals had rhetoric on their side, but so the devil often does; clever words are his stock-in-trade.

Sometimes they will be flattering words. He will pamper our intellectual pride, making us feel how exciting it is to listen to such a gifted, highly-qualified exponent of avant-garde thought. 'What on earth did I ever see in that old-fashioned conservative theology I used to believe? These new ideas are what intelligent Christians in the modern world are talking about. And by listening to this wonderful person, I can join their elevated ranks ...'

Sometimes they will be distorted words. He will use the vocabulary of biblical Christianity, but as he uses it he will subtly redefine his terms, so that the biblical words no longer convey their biblical meaning. Clearly, this was going on in Corinth. The false apostles talked about 'the Spirit', 'the gospel', 'Jesus' – cardinal words in

Christian vocabulary. But the content they put into those words was different. It was a different gospel, a different spirit, a different Jesus. So they confused the Corinthians by communicating false-hood behind a facade of orthodoxy.

That, of course, is why the church over the course of history has had to refine her creeds. In the days of the primitive church, it was sufficient simply to say: 'Jesus is Lord'. Such a confession was unambiguously Christian. But then along came the deceiver, preaching a different Jesus, and it was no longer enough to say, 'Jesus is Lord' because you had to answer the question: 'Which Jesus do you mean?' As errors of distortion became more subtle, so the creeds had to become more developed. But no matter how precise you make your statement of faith, there will always be some false teacher around who will construe a way in which he affirms it and yet means something different by it. So do not be deceived by distorted words. Orthodox language can mask demonic lies.

But the chief lesson that we learn from this passage is not to be fooled by mere words. What these pseudo-apostles demonstrate more clearly than anything else is that you do not need to be an outspoken heretic to be false to the gospel. If my suspicions are correct, the doctrinal credentials of these men were unimpeachable. It was not possible to tie down their error in terms of credal propositions they affirmed or denied. For what was wrong about them was that they had surrendered to the secular mood, and as a result their idea of Christian spirituality was awry. It showed in their methodology of evangelism, in the emphases in their preaching, in their style of leadership. As we have seen, it was unbalanced rather than heretical. They played down the cross, and played up the glory. But for Paul, such imbalance was still enough to put them into the devil's camp.

Worldliness is not the same as false teaching. Worldliness in fact can and often does exist in churches which are genuinely orthodox in their beliefs; because worldliness is not the result of having no cross in your theology, it is the result of not being prepared to have a cross in your life.

Mere words are not enough. A Christian leader can be using all the right words, and even mean the right things by those words, but still be communicating a different Jesus because his lifestyle speaks louder than what he is saying with his lips.

If you want to avoid the perils of Christian gullibility, here is the first lesson to learn from this passage. Do not be fooled by words.

(b) Do not be naive about money

It is clear that Paul regarded the way in which his evangelistic work was financed as enormously important. He took great pains to maintain a firm policy in this matter, and wisely so for two distinct reasons.

First, because money can corrupt a preacher. If you want to identify a questionable sect or group in the Christian world, look at their accounts. See where the money comes from and where it goes. Do not be surprised if you get some nasty shocks! Successful religion is big business, and there are plenty in the twentieth century, as there were in the first, who are willing to exploit the religious market. One obvious reason why Paul refused to take money from the Corinthian church was because he was determined not to be categorised with such peddlers of pop religion. It was important to the dignity of his apostolic office that the Corinthians should see him as someone who had offered the gospel to them without motives of personal financial gain. He was a preacher, not a salesman, and he wanted to make that absolutely clear to them.

Of course, Paul was willing to receive financial support for his ministry. But he was not prepared to accept fees for evangelistic services rendered. For that not only can corrupt the preacher, it can also alter the way people perceive the preacher. I remember an experience that brought this home to me very early in my Christian life while visiting on the Suffolk coast. One afternoon I stopped to watch the Punch and Judy show on the beach; it was quite a good show, and a fine crowd had gathered to watch it that sunny day. At the end of the show the puppeteer came round asking for contributions, and I remember very clearly how startled I was to see that the box he was shaking to receive people's monetary gifts was absolutely identical to the offering boxes we used in my home church.

Could there be a connection, I suddenly thought to myself? Could it be that some in my home church put money in the offering box with the same kind of attitude that this Punch and Judy man's audience was putting money into his box? As a tribute to the quality of his performance? As a payment for half-an-hour's good entertainment? As a gesture of charity to an impecunious street artist?

For precisely this reason, Paul would rather maintain his amateur status. He did not want people thinking of themselves as his clients. If a preacher is not willing to preach for nothing, he had better not preach at all. Once you see preaching as a 'professional' career you are halfway to not being a preacher any more but just a puppeteer who will say the kind of things that keep the audience happy and the cash-till ringing.

(c) Do not be sentimental about tolerance

You may feel Paul's verdict on his opponents as 'false apostles' and 'deceitful workmen' is unnecessarily severe, even bigoted. After all, anyone can make a mistake. A pedantic theologian could identify at least a dozen heretical statements in the average Christian prayer-meeting! Surely Paul is not showing much Christian love in stigmatising these rivals of his in this dreadful way?

If that is how you feel about it, maybe you should ask the question, 'What are the limits of my Christian tolerance?' Paul was persuaded that his critics were not innocently-deluded Christian brothers and sisters, nor even representatives of a different Christian tradition. They were agents of the devil; their invasion of Corinth was part of a demonic plot to destroy the church by subversion and sabotage. What kind of people do you believe might belong to that kind of category today? Or, in complaining of Paul's bigotry, are we really saying that we do not believe that any such category of demonic infiltration really exists? Are we saying that Paul is exaggerating the spiritual danger in which the church lies?

When some speak of Christian love, I fear it might be more accurate to speak instead of fatuous sentimentality, for that is what they are exhibiting. Sentimentality is undiscriminating love, and Christian love cannot be that. Genuine Christian tolerance is a virtue born of a strong conviction that the truth will vindicate itself. Modern humanistic tolerance is a vice, born of mass indecision about the truth, and which dare not confess any particular belief for fear of being accused of narrow-mindedness.

George Mikes puts it well in his book *How to be an Alien*. Today, he says, it is bad manners to assert anything confidently. It may be your personal view that two and two make four, but you must not state it in a self-assured way, because this is a democratic country and others may be of a different opinion. He is mocking, of course, but do you not see the element of truth in what he says? Pluralistic confusion has nothing to do with tolerance at all, still less with the strong virtue of Christian love. Paul loved these Corinthians; he tells us so in verse 11. But that did not stop him identifying the servants of Satan in their midst and denouncing them. On the contrary, it was his love for them that demanded such a denuncia-tion. 'I am jealous for you,' he says, 'with a godly jealousy.' This father in Christ could not stand idly by and see his daughter being seduced without protest. There were limits to his tolerance. There must be limits to our tolerance too. It will not do to be sentimental about the subject.

The most important things are not the things about which men are agreed, but those for which men will fight. Undoubtedly it is possible to fight over trivia, and the church has suffered such unnecessary belligerence. But it is a far greater mistake to refuse to fight at all. Be a pacifist about nuclear weapons if you wish, but please do not be passive about the truth. We are not in the kind of world that humanistic optimism wants us to believe in. All men are not struggling unitedly after the truth. There is a liar abroad with a vested interest in propagating untruth. Resist him, and do not be sentimental about tolerance.

They called Paul an amateur loudmouth. In a sense, that is all he was. But he fathered churches, and I suggest to you that he fathered them because he had convictions, convictions he was willing to fight for and was not prepared to see denied. He fathered churches because, man of love though he was, there were limits to his Christian tolerance. And in a world like ours, where bishops deny the Apostles' Creed, where ecumenical councils mouth Marxist slogans, where TV evangelists become millionaires, where pseudo-Christian cults often claim more adherents than mainstream Christian denominations – it behoves us all not to be fooled by words, not to be naive about money, not to be sentimental about tolerance, and above all, not to be gullible.

12
The Clown who Glimpsed Heaven
(2 Corinthians 11:16-12:10)

I repeat: Let no one take me for a fool. But if you do, then receive me just as you would a fool, so that I may do a little boasting. In this self-confident boasting I am not talking as the Lord would, but as a fool. Since many are boasting in the way the world does, I too will boast. You gladly put up with fools since you are so wise! In fact, you even put up with anyone who enslaves you or exploits you or takes advantage of you or pushes himself forward or slaps you in the face. To my shame I admit that we were too weak for that!

What anyone dares to boast about – I am speaking as a fool – I also dare to boast about. Are they Hebrews? So am I. Are they Israelites? So am I. Are they Abraham's descendants? So am I. Are they servants of Christ? (I am out of my mind to talk like this.) I am more. I have worked much harder, been in prison more frequently, been flogged more severely, and been exposed to death again and again. Five times I received from the Jews the forty lashes minus one. Three times I was beaten with rods, once I was stoned, three times I was shipwrecked, I spent a night and a day in the open sea, I have been constantly on the move. I have been in danger from rivers, in danger from bandits, in danger from my own countrymen, in danger from Gentiles; in danger in the city, in danger in the country, in danger at sea; and in danger from false brothers. I have laboured and toiled and have often gone without sleep; I have known hunger and thirst and have often gone without food; I have been cold and naked. Besides everything else, I face daily the pressure of my concern for all the churches. Who is weak, and I do not feel weak? Who is led into sin, and I do not inwardly burn?

If I must boast, I will boast of the things that show my weakness. The God and Father of the Lord Jesus, who is to be praised forever, knows that I am not lying. In Damascus the governor under King Aretas had the city of the Damascenes guarded in order to arrest me. But I was lowered in a basket from a window in the wall and slipped through his hands.

I must go on boasting. Although there is nothing to be gained, I will go on to visions and revelations from the Lord. I know a man in Christ who fourteen years ago was caught up to the third heaven. Whether it was in the body or out of the body I do not know – God knows. And I know that this man – whether in the body or apart from the body I do not know, but God knows – was caught up to paradise. He heard inexpressible things, things that man is not permitted to tell. I will boast about a man like that, but I will not boast about myself, except about my weaknesses. Even if I should choose to boast, I would not be a fool, because I would be speaking the truth. But I refrain, so no one will think more of me than is warranted by what I do or say.

To keep me from becoming conceited because of these surpassingly great revelations, there was given me a thorn in my flesh, a messenger of Satan, to torment me. Three times I pleaded with the Lord to take it away from me. But he said to me, "My grace is sufficient for you, for my power is made perfect in weakness." Therefore I will boast all the more gladly about my weaknesses, so that Christ's power may rest on me. That is why, for Christ's sake, I delight in weaknesses, in insults, in hardships, in persecutions, in difficulties. For when I am weak, then I am strong (2 Corinthians 11:16-12:10).

I WANT TO TALK IN THIS CHAPTER ABOUT THE DANGERS OF BEING TOO SPIRITUAL. You may feel that is a rather unexpected and even reprehensible thing to want to talk about. Surely, it should be every Christian's ambition to be as spiritual as possible? Nevertheless I feel I am on strong ground writing about this subject, because in this letter the apostle Paul is dealing at Corinth with precisely the kind of super-spirituality I want to warn you against. And it is quite clear that he thought it was dangerous too.

Paul's apostolic credentials were being made to look decidedly dubious. We saw in the last chapter how he was stung into sarcasm by the accusation that he was just an amateur loudmouth. But that was not the end of the problem. Even more damning than the amateurism of Paul's rhetoric, his whole image and persona were too ordinary for the taste of some of his critics. He was too normal.

You may ask what is so wrong with being normal. Well, Paul was a religious leader. He was supposed to be a very spiritual man. And Greeks entertained certain expectations of such a person.

A religious leader ought to be a superior kind of human being, magical, semi-divine even. Maybe he will have achieved great exploits like the heroes of Greek mythology – a dynamic Hercules who emerges from all kinds of trials and difficulties of life victorious and unscathed. Or maybe he will have psychic visions or occult experiences like the famous oracles of the classical age, or the priests of the newly popular mystery religions.

At the very least, anybody who was going to be a credible religious leader in Greek society had to be powerful . The Greeks despised bodily weakness of any kind, believing it to be quite incompatible with divinity. So a hero had to be physically a specimen of perfection. If he did not have the body of an athlete, at least he had to project an image of health and vigour. But more than that he had to have a strong and dynamic personality. He had to be self-confident, even a little arrogant. Humility was not a virtue for the Greeks. For them, humility was indistinguishable from servility; it was a vice. A great man had to be able to boast; he had to be self-assertive; he had to be proud. This is what it meant to be great.

Paul simply did not conform, as his rivals were keen to point out. 'Paul? He may seem quite intimidating when he writes letters but in the flesh he is a weak ineffectual little man. Supernatural? But there are rumours he's had a recurring illness. How can he be an apostle? Spirituality means power, and Paul is weak! So he isn't spiritual – not as spiritual as us, anyway!'

It was this, as we have seen, that motivated Paul to write the whole of this letter, and particularly its final chapters. It was not that he was upset for his own sake. These pseudo-apostles, as he sarcastically calls them, were not just injuring his personal reputation, they were doing something far worse. Though superficially orthodox in their doctrine and apparently impeccable in their Christian credentials, by projecting this secularised, worldly image of what it means to be spiritual they were subtly subverting Christianity itself. Under the cloak of being more spiritual than Paul, they were actually offering people a false Jesus; a Jesus who no longer suffered, who no longer carried a cross, who was no longer weak enough to be born in a manger. And that, Paul simply could not allow.

He had to puncture the self-inflated egos of these rivals; he had to expose their claims of super-spirituality as erroneous. He had to show the rank-and-file Christians at Corinth that these so-called apostles could only portray him as unspiritual because they had a totally wrong idea of what real spirituality was. And since they had chosen to make Paul himself the focus of their mistaken ideas, he had no alternative but to use himself as an object lesson to correct them.

It is quite clear that these were uncomfortable chapters for Paul to write. Talking about himself felt like bragging, which did not come naturally to him. It made him feel, he tells us, like a fool. But the confusion of the Corinthians left him with no choice. He would have to 'boast', just as if he were one of those puffed-up worldly pseudo-apostles who were enjoying the limelight in Corinth so much. But, he tells them, he will do so only under protest.

> **Let no-one take me for a fool. But if you do, then receive me just as you would a fool, so that I may do a little boasting (11:16).**

In other words: 'It seems that to gain a hearing from you lot, one has to behave like a braggart. Well, I will play along with your silly game and blow my own trumpet like a clown for a while, if that is what you want.' But ...

> **In this self-confident boasting I am not talking as the Lord would, but as a fool. Since many are boasting in the way the world does, I too will boast. You gladly put up with fools since you are so wise! (11:17-19).**

We have noticed in previous chapters how Paul uses irony to debunk his rivals. He is doing the same here. 'I know you will condescend to tolerate this little fit of insanity on my part, he says – you all being so eminently sane!' After all, my little exhibition of egocentricity is nothing compared to that gang of bullies to whom you seem so anxious to kow-tow at the moment!

> **In fact, you even put up with any one who enslaves you or exploits you or takes advantage of you or pushes himself forward or slaps you in the face (11:20).**

Here is an insight into the kind of authoritarian model of Christian leadership that the false apostles were establishing at Corinth, with its typically Greek contempt for the underling and its expectation of grovelling submission from those not privileged to belong to their spiritual elite. 'No,' says Paul – the sarcasm dripping with bitterness –

> **To my shame I admit that we were too weak for that! (11:21).**

However, if the Corinthians want to know what Paul's claims to be spiritual are, he is reluctantly prepared to set them out. Genetics, for a start. Greeks were particularly interested in a person's ethnic origins. Here is Paul's pedigree, then.

> **Are they Hebrews? So am I. Are they Israelites? So am I.**
> **Are they Abraham's descendants? So am I** (11:22).

Reading between the lines it appears likely that Paul's rivals were
Jews trying to capitalise upon their Palestinian identity. In a place
like Corinth, a touch of the exotic in your background was a decided
advantage. Eastern religions were considered very avant-garde,
much as they are in some circles today. Paul assures the Corinthians
that if they are foolish enough to think they are more likely to get
religious experiences through Jews than anybody else, his ethnic
origin is every bit as superior as that of his rivals. He is also a Jew:
one hundred per cent born and bred.

What about heroic exploits?

> **Are they servants of Christ? (I am out of my mind to talk like**
> **this.) I am more. I have worked much harder, been in prison**
> **more frequently, been flogged more severely, and been**
> **exposed to death again and again. Five times I received from**
> **the Jews the forty lashes minus one. Three times I was**
> **beaten with rods, once I was stoned, three times I was**
> **shipwrecked, I spent a night and a day in the open sea. I have**
> **been constantly on the move. I have been in danger from**
> **rivers, in danger from bandits ... in danger from false**
> **brothers. I have laboured and toiled and have often gone**
> **without sleep; I have known hunger and thirst and have**
> **often gone without food; I have been cold and naked. Besides**
> **everything else, I face daily the pressure of my concern for**
> **all the churches** (11:23-28).

This catalogue is the real master stroke. Greek heroes were sometimes eulogised by this kind of curriculum vitae. But see what Paul
is doing. What things does he include in his catalogue of achievements? The results of his great preaching crusades? Not mentioned.
The prolific output of his theological pen? Not a word. His daring
enterprise and missionary initiative? Well, a little bit of the adventure comes through; but not much positive is said about it. The long
list of impressive names of influential Christian apostles that he

knew personally? Not included. He lists nothing, in fact, that would be in the least impressive by Greek standards. Instead, he lists the persecutions, the dangers and the crippling sense of responsibility that pressured him every minute of every day.

'And how,' says Paul, 'do I cope with all these troubles, deprivations and anxieties?' Does he emerge like some young Hercules, fresh and glowing with self-confidence at the end of each test? Not at all!

> **Who is weak, and I do not feel weak? Who is led into sin, and I do not inwardly burn?** (11:29).

Some commentators, it is true, take this verse as a development of verse 28 arguing that Paul is explaining the nature of the worry he has for the churches. If there is some failure or apostasy it affects him personally. If someone is wobbly in their stand for Christ, he is debilitated by it. If someone falls away from the truth, he burns with indignation or embarrassment. That interpretation makes good sense, but it seems more likely that in this context Paul is identifying his *own* moral and spiritual frailty. He is saying, 'Apostle as I am, I am not sufficient for all these things. I am not stronger than anybody else. I am no more impervious to temptation than anybody else. My only testimony, as a result of all these trials in the Christian ministry, is to an ever-deepening sense of personal inadequacy.'

> **If I must boast, I will boast of the things that show my weakness. The God and Father of the Lord Jesus, who is to be praised forever, knows that I am not lying** (11:30-31).

And while on the subject of his record, Paul adds a postscript, 'If they really want to know what sort of apostle I am, I am the sort who when the going gets really tough, runs away. It is true, I have always been like it. The very first thing I did after I was baptised was to run away.'

> **In Damascus the governor under King Aretas had the city of the Damascenes guarded in order to arrest me. But I was**

> **lowered in a basket from a window in the wall and slipped through his hands** (11:32-33).

That is Paul for you! Not a courageous Alexander, who climbs into enemy fortresses in order to capture them. No: Paul is the sort who climbs out of enemy fortresses in order to avoid getting captured himself. 'A coward, that is what I am,' says Paul! 'I do not deny it.'

See what Paul is trying to do here? He is turning upside down the glamorous image of Christian spirituality that the Corinthians were being fed by the false teachers. They thought of an apostle as a dynamic superman exuding success in all directions. But they were wrong. People who present themselves in that kind of boastful manner, Paul says, just give themselves away as false apostles. For real apostles of Christ are those who experience persecution and contempt from the world. They experience danger born of an unfriendly providence, they experience privation born of abject poverty, they experience anxiety born of intolerable responsibility; and most of all, they experience mortification born of the knowledge of their own unworthiness and inadequacy. If they insist upon Paul blowing his own trumpet like a fool, he will do so. But it is things like this he will parade in front of them. Unlike the leaders they admire so much, Paul does not despise weakness. He empathises with it. And if he has to boast, he will boast of the things that demonstrate his weakness.

What about supernatural experiences? After all, you expect great religious leaders to go in for them too, don't you?

> **I must go on boasting. Although there is nothing to be gained, I will go on to visions and revelations from the Lord. I know a man in Christ who fourteen years ago was caught up to the third heaven. Whether it was in the body or out of the body, I do not know – God knows... He heard inexpressible things, things that man is not permitted to tell. I will boast about a man like that, but I will not boast about myself, except about my weaknesses** (12:1-2, 4-5).

What we have here is quite clearly a description of a profound, ecstatic or mystical experience. It may be that modesty forbids Paul speaking of it in the first person, even though he is speaking 'as a fool'. Or it may be that the experience was so divorced from Paul's normal life that it felt as though it happened to another person. But it is clear that Paul is not telling us second-hand about the experience of some friend (see verse 7). The 'man in Christ' was none other than himself.

There are several things worth noting.

The first is that even for Paul, such mystical experience was *extremely rare*. It happened 'fourteen years ago'. So this was a once-in-a-lifetime experience, not a regular feature of Paul's daily quiet time.

Secondly, it was *extraordinarily vivid*; 'whether in the body or out of the body'. In other words, he felt himself caught up into direct experience of the spiritual realms, what he calls the 'third heaven'. Whether it was an intrapsychic vision or an actual physical rapture, he could not be sure; it was so vivid. It completely eclipsed all normal consciousness.

Thirdly, Paul makes clear that such experience was *very special*, and did provide, potentially at least, grounds for some measure of spiritual pride. 'About a man like that I will boast.' This is not normal Christian experience. A man who experiences such a thing has been marked out as specially privileged.

Fourthly, Paul regards this experience as *peculiarly personal and private*. He heard inexpressible things, he says, things that 'man is not permitted to tell'. So it was not given for Paul to share with others. It was private between him and the Lord. For a start it was impossible to share it. Like all mystical experiences it defied description. More than that, he says, it would have been illegitimate to try to share it. The mystery involved was too sacred; it was not intended for public declaration.

Furthermore, Paul says it would have been imprudent to share it.

Even if I should choose to boast [in other words, to talk about

> this thing], I would not be a fool, because I would be speaking
> the truth. But I refrain, so no one will think more of me than
> is warranted by what I do or say (12:6).

This is extremely important. Paul did not want to influence what
people thought of him by exhibiting this experience. It was personal, it could not be verified. If he had boasted about it, he would
have opened the door to all kinds of charlatans who deceitfully
boasted of similarly unverifiable, mystical experiences and claimed
authority in the church on the basis of them. So Paul refused to
bolster his prestige in that fashion. He preferred his reputation to be
based only on those things that could be unambiguously corrobo-
rated by observation of his character and his teachings: 'what I do
and say' is all he wants people to respect him for, not his dramatic
visions and revelations.

The fifth matter worth noting about this mystical experience is
this: it was *not without cost*.

> To keep me from becoming conceited because of these
> surpassingly great revelations, there was given me a thorn
> in my flesh, a messenger of Satan, to torment me (12:7).

There has been speculation for centuries as to what Paul meant
precisely by the 'thorn in the flesh'. Probably it was some kind of
physical ailment. But the important thing is not the nature of this
handicap, but its effect on Paul's ministry. Why was it given him?
To stop him 'becoming conceited'.

There was a real danger associated with the spiritual privilege of
these mystical revelations: the danger of pride. The thorn in the
flesh was a prophylactic remedy against such a temptation. Notice
how Paul responded to it.

> Three times I pleaded with the Lord to take it away from me
> (12:8).

Paul was not willing to accept this thorn. It is not an overstatement

to say he was rebellious. But notice how, finally, he was reconciled
to it.

> **But he said to me, "My grace is sufficient for you, for my
> power is made perfect in weakness"** (12:9).

God would not take the risk of removing the thorn. It had a vital
purpose in Paul's life. What he did do was to assure Paul that no
hindrance would be suffered in his ministry as a result of it; on the
contrary, he would be all the more effective. Others would become
Christians not because they saw Paul as some impressive, dynamic,
supernatural hero, but because the grace of God could be seen at
work in him, despite his natural weakness. And Paul came at the end
to recognise that was the best way.

So here is Paul the clown: but the clown who glimpsed heaven.
His answer to these rivals who accused him of being unspiritual is
not to try and compete with them but, by a blend of irony and
paradox, to show them that their ideas of spirituality and his were
poles apart. 'It simply is not true,' he says, 'to say that to be spiritual
is to project an image of superiority and supernaturalism and power.
On the contrary, real spirituality looks ordinary; real spirituality
looks weak; even as Christ looked weak and ordinary as he lay in the
manger and as he hung on the cross.'

These verses are of enormous relevance to us, for the kind of
super-spirituality that Paul is countering is very far from absent in our
twentieth century. There are plenty of Christian leaders today who
want to surround themselves with similar kinds of supernatural aura,
who feel that to be spiritual must mean miracles, visions and 'power'.

Note carefully, then, Paul's insistence that not everything we
experience of Christ is necessarily to be shared. There are intimate
details of our devotional life which, like the intimate details of our
marital life, are cheapened by public exposure. Be suspicious of
people who are always shouting their mouth off about the revelations they have had; for reticence in such matters is a mark of real
spirituality.

Notice also that ecstatic experiences are supernormal, even for Christians. From Paul's account it is clear that such experiences can be authentic. We are not to label mystics as demonically inspired or self-deluded. But mystical experience should not be the basis for evaluating a person's spirituality. Claims to this kind of experience can be misleading. Deeds and words were what mattered, not psychic ecstasies.

That's why Paul did not seek after such experiences. His 'third heaven' encounter just happened to him, out of the blue. It was not the result of any kind of mystical discipline. He had not prayed for months on end, fasting in the desert. It just happened to him, and never happened again as far as we know. Even in the greatest saints, such experiences are rare, or totally absent: because it is character, not experience, that really shows the mark of the Spirit in someone's life. Listen to these words from St John of the Cross, one of the greatest Christian mystics of all time:

> All visions, revelations, heavenly feelings, and whatever is greater than these, are not worth the least act of humility, being the fruits of that charity which neither values nor seeks itself, which thinketh well not of self, but of others. Many souls to whom visions have never come, are incomparably more advanced in the way of perfection than others to whom many have been given.

Notice too Paul's testimony that *the prayers of the greatest saints are sometimes not answered in the way they want*. Three times Paul asked for something and three times God said, 'No'. Take comfort from that! Contrary to pagan ideas, prayer is not a magic wish granted unconditionally by some kind of fairy godmother; it is a gracious gift from a caring God. And there is no way that the caring Father-God is going to give us something he knows is not good for us, no matter how long we badger him for it. Even Jesus prayed once, 'Take this cup from me,' and got the answer, 'No.' Thank goodness, God sometimes says 'No'! Aren't you glad your parents sometimes said 'No'?

This is particularly relevant in the whole debate about miraculous healing. Suffering is something Christians must be prepared to accept for the positive contribution it can sometimes make to their lives as Paul had to accept his thorn in the flesh. Some people tell us that we have a right to be healed and that if we are sick and are not healed, there must be something spiritually wrong with us. It is not so. There is an expectation of suffering in the Christian life. Of course, we pray for relief: but if our prayers are persistently declined, then we must eventually conclude that God is saying to us, 'You are more useful to me with suffering than without it.' There are qualities that we learn by means of suffering, and that we learn no other way. Even Christ, we are told, was 'made perfect through suffering' (Heb. 2:10). God's grace in us is sometimes only brought to its peak of fulfilment through an experience of crippling weakness.

Incidentally, do you observe that Paul draws no sharp line between Satan's work and God's will in this matter. He calls this thorn in the flesh, which God had given him, 'a messenger of Satan'. You might have thought anything 'satanic' was bound to be an appropriate object for 'deliverance' ministry. But not so. Satan is under God's control, and sometimes God gives him some opportunity in us, as in the case of Job. Paul was a better man because of his thorn in the flesh. As far as God was concerned, a little physical discomfort was a small price to pay for the conquest of ego in this servant of his.

But the final thing I want you to notice is the great lesson which Paul learned.

> **Therefore I will boast all the more gladly about my weaknesses, so that Christ's power may rest on me. That is why, for Christ's sake, I delight in weaknesses, in insults, in hardships, in persecutions, in difficulties** [in other words: in all these things with which your Greek frame of mind you find so hard to associate with being spiritual]. **For when I am weak, then I am strong** (12:9-10).

It is hard to exaggerate the importance of those verses. They represent the very kernel of Paul's thesis in these final chapters. They are the final rebuke to the Corinthian mind-set. It is the Corinthians, he is saying, who are the fools. They admire those who boast of their revelations and their visions. They grovel before those who brag of their achievements. But Paul does not: and it was a direct result of the intensity of his own apostolic visions and revelations that he learned that Christianity is incompatible with such behaviour. Christian spirituality delights in weakness; because only in the acceptance and confession of weakness does he find the supernatural grace of God flowing to meet his need.

Here is the paradox of the cross: that only in humiliation do we find God exalting us, only in dying do we find God making us alive, only in throwing our lives away do we find God giving life back to us. Only when I am weak, am I strong.

13
Profile of an Apostle
(2 Corinthians 12:11-13:14)

I have made a fool of myself, but you drove me to it. I ought to have been commended by you, for I am not in the least inferior to the "super-apostles," even though I am nothing. The things that mark an apostle –signs, wonders and miracles – were done among you with great perseverance. How were you inferior to the other churches, except that I was never a burden to you? Forgive me this wrong!

Now I am ready to visit you for the third time, and I will not be a burden to you, because what I want is not your possessions but you. After all, children should not have to save up for their parents, but parents for their children. So I will very gladly spend for you everything I have and expend myself as well. If I love you more, will you love me less? Be that as it may, I have not been a burden to you. Yet, crafty fellow that I am, I caught you by trickery! Did I exploit you through any of the men I sent you? I urged Titus to go to you and I sent our brother with him. Titus did not exploit you, did he? Did we not act in the same spirit and follow the same course?

Have you been thinking all along that we have been defending ourselves to you? We have been speaking in the sight of God as those in Christ; and everything we do, dear friends, is for your strengthening. For I am afraid that when I come I may not find you as I want you to be, and you may not find me as you want me to be. I fear that there may be quarrelling, jealousy, outbursts of anger, factions, slander, gossip, arrogance and disorder. I am afraid that when I come again my God will humble me before you, and I will be grieved over many who have sinned earlier and have not repented of the impurity, sexual sin and debauchery in which they have indulged.

This will be my third visit to you. "Every matter must be established by the testimony of two or three witnesses." I already gave you a warning when I was with you the second time. I now repeat it while absent: On my return I will not spare those who sinned earlier or any of the others, since you are demanding proof that Christ is speaking through me. He is not weak in dealing with you, but is powerful among you. For to be sure, he was crucified in weakness, yet he lives by God's power. Likewise, we are weak in him, yet by God's power we will live with him to serve you.

Examine yourselves to see whether you are in the faith; test yourselves. Do you not realise that Christ Jesus is in you – unless, of course, you fail the test? And I trust that you will discover that we have not failed the test. Now we pray to God that you will not do anything wrong. Not that people will see that we have stood the test but that you will do what is right even though we may seem to have failed. For we cannot do anything against the truth, but only for the truth. We are glad whenever we are weak but you are strong; and our prayer is for your perfection. This is why I write these things when I am absent, that when I come I may not have to be harsh in my use of authority – the authority the Lord gave me for building you up, not for tearing you down.

Finally, brothers, good-bye. Aim for perfection, listen to my appeal, be of one mind, live in peace. And the God of love and peace will be with you.

Greet one another with a holy kiss. All the saints send their greetings. May the grace of the Lord Jesus Christ, and the love of God, and the fellowship of the Holy Spirit be with you all (2 Corinthians 12:11-13:14).

PAUL HATED HAVING TO BLOW HIS OWN TRUMPET. As far as he was concerned, bragging was the mark of a fool, but since no-one else would speak up for him, it seemed he had no alternative.

> I have made a fool of myself, but you drove me to it. I ought to have been commended by you, for I am not in the least inferior to the "super-apostles,'" even though I am nothing (12:11).

He is, I think, quoting the word that his critics used of him – 'a nothing', a nobody. He freely acknowledges the title. Whatever he has done has been done by the grace of God – not least his triumph over the 'thorn in the flesh'. Nevertheless, he assures the Corinthians, he is not prepared to be regarded as subordinate to the spiritual elite who are gaining ground among them in Corinth. For God has called him, 'nothing' though he is, to be an apostle.

The Corinthians more than anyone else should recognise that, because it was through his ministry that the church was planted there in Corinth. He ought to be commended by them; but since they refuse to defend his apostolic office, no false modesty is going to prevent him from defending it himself. On the contrary, in this final section, he enumerates three characteristics of true apostleship and lays claim to them: endurance, integrity and authority.

1. Paul's endurance

> The things that mark an apostle – signs, wonders and miracles – were done among you with great perseverance (12:12).

This is an important verse for two reasons. First, it provides an important background for the way we evaluate miracles in the New Testament. It seems to make clear that in many cases, miracles were designed to authenticate the apostles in the special role they had to play in the purpose of God. If you look at the book of Acts, this is sometimes made quite explicit. Luke tells us that the *apostles* did great signs. He deliberately narrows it down to them. This does not mean that others did not work miracles; clearly they did. Nor does it mean that the age of miracles is now passed. But there are grounds for seeing in verse 12 a clear implication that the extraordinary quality and quantity of supernatural events that we find in the book of Acts was a special feature of the apostolic age. The apostles were supernaturally endowed in a way that a pastor or missionary today is not.

But the other reason this verse is important is that it makes it clear that miracles were not the only, or even the chief, characteristic even of apostles. That is why he says, 'These things ... were done among you with great perseverance.' This could, I suppose, be interpreted as 'I performed miracles perseveringly' though it sounds rather odd. In the light of what Paul has been saying in Chapters 11 and 12, however, another interpretation is more likely: namely that alongside his miracles there was another characteristic of Paul's ministry when he was in Corinth, which was even more distinctly apostolic: perseverance. 'These things that mark an apostle – signs, wonders and miracles – were done among you'; but something else was shown too: endurance.

'I had a hard time in Corinth,' says Paul. 'I was scared, I was in danger of my life. Those months I spent with you were times of immense stress. And you saw me, in my personal frailty, cope with that stress. And that is the mark of an apostle no less than the signs, wonders and miracles that these "super-apostles" of yours like to boast about so much.' Paul's signs and wonders were not just flashy exhibitions of Christian showmanship. They were born out of suffering and adversity. They happened in the context of a life stretched to the limits. If you seek the credentials of a Christian leader, that quality of perseverance is every bit as important as anything overtly supernatural.

Do not ask an apostle how many healings he has done. You would do better to ask first how many scars he bears. Do not ask how much magic he has up his sleeve – ask how much grit he demonstrates. For these are marks of Christian leadership. The way somebody copes with adversity is a better index of their spirituality than any number of entertaining stories regarding miraculously-answered prayers and the like.

2. Paul's integrity

> How were you inferior to the other churches, except that I
> was never a burden to you? Forgive me this wrong! Now I
> am ready to visit you for the third time, and I will not be a
> burden to you, because what I want is not your possessions
> but you. After all, children should not have to save up for
> their parents, but parents for their children (12:13-14).

You will recall the slanders the false teachers had uttered against Paul:
deriving from his failure to charge fees. He was either a mere amateur,
unfitted for the office he was trying to fulfil, or a con-man with some
crafty scheme in mind. Paul makes reference to both these allegations
as he speaks here. 'Does that make me inferior?' he demands, clearly
referring to the first allegation, and later he says, 'Crafty fellow that
I am, I caught you by trickery!' (verse 16) – alluding to the second.
He is quite emphatic that such charges are completely unfounded.
'Why,' he says, 'I see myself as your spiritual father.' Would a father
demand payment for parental services rendered to his children? No
more can he demand payment from them. If occasion demanded it,
he would sacrifice himself totally for their welfare.

> So I will very gladly spend for you everything I have and
> expend myself as well. If I love you more, will you love me
> less? (12:15).

Of course, Paul is not saying that it is wrong for teaching elders in
the church to be paid by the church. He makes it clear elsewhere that
it is perfectly allowable. But he is implying that there are circumstances where a preacher is wiser not to take money from a congregation, to ensure his integrity is above suspicion. We would do well
to always ask the question, when assessing people who offer themselves to us as Christian leaders: How anxious are they to pass the
hat round? How important to them are the financial aspects of the
office? Paul wants to warn us that there are so-called 'leaders'
around, who are more interested in exploiting than in serving.

3. Paul's authority

But the chief emphasis in this passage is upon Paul's personal authority to discipline the church.

> **Have you been thinking all along that we have been defending ourselves to you? (12:19).**

We could be forgiven for thinking that that was precisely what he has been doing! But Paul says that rightly understood, it is not what he has been doing at all.

> **We have been speaking in the sight of God as those in Christ; and everything we do, dear friends, is for your strengthening. For I am afraid that when I come I may not find you as I want you to be, and you may not find me as you want me to be (12:19-20).**

Paul's cancellation of his proposed visit to Corinth had fuelled his opponents' claims that he was basically a rather weak person: 'See, he can't face you.' But Paul insists, in these closing lines of his letter, that he is now determined to come to Corinth. He would delay no longer, and when he arrived they were going to find a rather different man from the one some of them have been expecting. Perhaps they may have deduced from his earlier chapters that he saw himself in the dock with them as the jury, and that he was trying to secure a 'not guilty' verdict from them?

'Not so,' says Paul. His self-defence has been conducted not because he felt any need of their approval but because he knew they needed his help. 'It is for your strengthening, not for my own prestige or to protect my reputation that I come. My concern is not to win your verdict but to contribute to your welfare. For it is you Corinthians who are in the dock,' he says, 'not me.'

'You Corinthians are in trouble, and unless you respect me, I can do nothing to help you. As God is my judge,' Paul is saying, 'I am an apostle; and if you do not realise that and respect me, then I shall be forced to prove it to you in a way I do not really want to; by exerting discipline in your church.'

It is possible that Paul has in mind the type of supernatural discipline that apostles sometimes invoked in New Testament times, as for example in the story of Ananias and Sapphira.

At the very least, he is threatening the excommunication of offenders. And in so doing, he is claiming a huge personal authority. That is something he has fought shy of doing all the way through this letter, preferring instead to use the weapons of irony and sarcasm. But in these final verses, he speaks candidly. The time for indirect approaches, for tact and discretion is past. The issue is serious: he has to spell out to them what the consequences will be if they do not respond to his appeal.

(1) The pain of discipline

It distressed Paul to contemplate church discipline in this way.

> **I fear that there may be quarrelling, jealousy, outbursts of anger, factions, slander, gossip, arrogance and disorder. I am afraid that when I come again my God will humble me before you, and I will be grieved over many who have sinned earlier and have not repented of the impurity, sexual sin and debauchery in which they have indulged (12:20-21).**

So many in positions of authority would gain a sense of malicious satisfaction from being able to exact public retribution from people who had offended them. The power complex is all too common. But that was not Paul's attitude at all. It genuinely hurt him to have to think about disciplinary action. He loved the church. It would be humiliating to him to discover the kind of immorality and dissension among them that he anticipated. It would humiliate him further to have to deal with it. Emotionally involved with them as he was, he felt that he would have tears to endure before Corinth would once again awaken smiles in him.

(2) The authority of discipline

This will be my third visit to you. "Every matter must be established by the testimony of two or three witnesses." I already gave you a warning when I was with you the second time. I now repeat it while absent: On my return I will not spare those who sinned earlier or any of the others (13:1-2).

It is not quite clear why Paul quotes Deuteronomy 19:15. He may be saying that when he comes he will be requiring, just as Moses did in the Old Testament law, that any offence be substantiated by witnesses. But it is more likely that he is quoting it rather loosely to imply, 'Look, I have already given you two warnings; this letter constitutes a third. Now you have no excuse. Judgment is going to follow.'

However you interpret the reference, it is clear that Paul was not prepared to tolerate gross sin in the church. It would pain him to have to exert his authority in a disciplinary way, but he was determined to do it. He had already postponed action because of the pain that he felt (as we know from Chapter 2). But he was not prepared to postpone the necessary moral surgery indefinitely.

(3) The cross at the heart of discipline

...Since you are demanding proof that Christ is speaking through me. He is not weak in dealing with you, but is powerful among you. For to be sure, he was crucified in weakness, yet he lives by God's power. Likewise, we are weak in him, yet by God's power we will live with him to serve you (13:3-4).

Paul summarises here the paradox of the cross which was, as we saw in the last chapter, the key to his apostolic ministry. 'The strange blend of humility and glory that characterised the Lord Jesus, crucified in weakness but raised in glory, is reflected in me. I have no ambition to make an impression, but impressive I will be, when God demonstrates his power through me against sinners in his church.'

They should not be deceived by his apparent weakness, any more than they should be deceived by the cross. Jesus was crucified, but out of that crucifixion came resurrection power: all authority in heaven and earth is given to me, says the risen Lord. And weak Paul will, by that same authority, deal with them. That is why he would much rather that they sorted themselves out before he got there.

> **Examine yourselves to see whether you are in the faith; test yourselves. Do you not realise that Christ Jesus is in you – unless, of course, you fail the test? (12:5)**

Of course, there have been periods in church history when the practice of self-examination has been emphasised to such a degree that it has become a rather morbid introspection. Luther suffered greatly from the torments of an excessively introvert spirituality in the days when he was a monk, and that may be one of the reasons why the Protestant tradition played down the role of subjectivism in Christian assurance. The Reformers taught that we should live simply on faith in God's promises, and not enquire too much of our consciences: such self-enquiry, they might even say, implies doubt in God. But you can carry that too far. For Christian assurance does require self-examination. We dare not claim to be a new creature in Christ unless we can demonstrate the fruit of it in our lives. It may well be that some go too far in that direction, making assurance so subjective as to be over dependent on feelings. That can be unhelpful, especially for people with very sensitive consciences who are never satisfied by what they find within themselves. But it does seem clear from what Paul is saying here that self-examination ought to be part of Christian devotional practice. For complacency is a trap into which it is easy to fall.

'Test yourselves,' he says, 'to see whether your character confirms your faith is the genuine article, that you are not just a plastic Christian putting on a show.' Paul does not encourage us to anticipate a pessimistic verdict about ourselves. But the possibility of hypocrisy must be given a mental airing. We dare not sweep the issue under the carpet. For it is possible to fail the test.

(4) Dealing with sin

Paul longed that these Corinthians would find the guts to be able to examine their own lives, and to deal with the sin, the immorality and the dissension that was torturing their church before he got there. Why? Because self-examination is far preferable to church discipline. Far better that we ensure that our spiritual walk is strong, than we should allow ourselves to go spiritually downhill or fall into some gross kind of sin, and then leave it to the pastor or the elders of the church to have to discipline or rebuke us.

That's what Paul means when he says, 'In all this discipline it is your welfare that is in my heart.' It is not a matter of Paul coming in and throwing his weight around in order to re-establish his sense of self-importance. He is not in the business of exercising draconian authority for its own sake.

> **And I trust that you will discover that we have not failed the test. Now we pray to God that you will not do anything wrong. Not that people will see that we have stood the test but that you will do what is right even though we may seem to have failed. For we cannot do anything against the truth, but only for the truth (13:6-8).**

It is rather difficult to untangle these verses with confidence. Essentially Paul is saying, 'I wish that you would recognise the authenticity of my apostolic office, that I "passed the test," and would therefore acknowledge the legitimacy of my authority among you and take appropriate steps to deal with these offenders before I come.'

> **We are glad whenever we are weak but you are strong; and our prayer is for your perfection. This is why I write these things when I am absent, that when I come I may not have to be harsh in my use of authority – the authority the Lord gave me for building you up, not for tearing you down (13:9-10).**

Paul is glad to have a reputation for weakness, if that means they are strong. His concern is for their maturity. What matters to him is not his reputation but their spiritual welfare. The authority God gave him was not to build himself up into some kind of super-apostle, it was to build them up into a Christian church worthy of the name.

Paul's farewell

> **Finally, brothers, good-bye. Aim for perfection, listen to my appeal, be of one mind, live in peace. And the God of love and peace will be with you (13:11).**

There is much that we could say out of this epistle that has application to us today, but perhaps there is no lesson more important for us to learn than this: that God is concerned about quality.

Everything you buy these days has to pass some kind of quality control, if it is a product worth buying. Well, God practises quality-control in the church. It is quite clear from this letter that numerical response was not the most important measure of evangelistic success. Paul was not content with immature, superficial Christians. He wanted converts who had a profound understanding of what it really meant to be a Christian. These Corinthians were in danger because they were becoming worldly in their thinking. They were mistaking secular success and power for spirituality. Paul could not allow them to get away with that.

Because in the wake of such false ideas of spirituality comes sin. Perhaps not immediately, but always eventually. In the wake of false ideas of spirituality, there come quarrelling, jealousy, anger, factions, slander, gossip, arrogance and disorder. Yes, and impurity, and sexual sin and debauchery too.

These things are all of a piece when Christians slide away from the pathway of the cross. Paul was desperate that the Corinthians should not do that. He teaches us as much by his example as by his words what it really means, to stay there at the foot of the cross. For only there can we learn the most vital and yet the most paradoxical lesson of all – *the strength of weakness*.